"'God must hate me.' If you've ever felt th
Elizabeth Hagan's beautiful new book. Nc
without also being helped to see their own st
important, to empathize more deeply with
dreams long deferred or permanently denied. This is the kind of book
you will always remember and be better for having read." —Brian D.
McLaren, Author/Activist

"With emotional depth and pastoral sensitivity, Elizabeth Hagan gives
particular insight to the visceral longing for biological motherhood.
Her story is instructive for people who are not aware of the trials of
infertility, and it is hopeful as Hagan bears witness for the countless
women and men who know those trials all too well." —Carol Howard
Merritt, Author of *Healing Spiritual Wounds*

"An utterly absorbing account of birthing—and allowing God to
birth—compassion, pain, hope, solidarity, abundance, and lament.
But not only those: in this birth story, what's born is a richness in the
spiritual life, and, ultimately, a self. (Which means that you needn't
be, or want to be, a mother, to find this book good, wise company.)"
—Lauren F. Winner, Author of *Mudhouse Sabbath* and *Wearing God*

"Raw. Real. Funny. Honest. Hagan's tale of hope amid infertility will
delight readers with its accessibility and nourish them with thoughtful
reflections on love, faith and family." —MaryAnn McKibben Dana,
Author of *Sabbath in the Suburbs*

"As a fellow infertile, I wish my wife and I had this book during our
period of sorrow to provide language for our grief. I highly recommend
this book to pastors, therapists, chaplains or anyone who is willing
to be present with those who are suffering." —Todd Maberry, Duke
Divinity School

"Elizabeth Hagan speaks intimately and powerfully to all who have
ever experienced the inability to fully realize a lifelong hope or
heartfelt dream. ... This book left me feeling refreshingly vulnerable
and incredibly inspired!" —Allen V. Harris, Regional Minister for the
Christian Church (Disciples Of Christ)

"*Birthed* is an unflinching, courageous, and much-needed portrait of what it means to wrestle faithfully with desire, death, and rebirth. By shying away from trite phrases and easy answers, *Birthed* invites us to reflect honestly and courageously on our own forays into the valley of the shadow of death. Yes, this is a story about one woman's hard-fought struggle through infertility, but it is also a much-needed reminder that God's Spirit is always making things new in us." —Maria A. Kane, Rector, St. Paul's Episcopal Church, Waldorf, Maryland

"In *Birthed*, Elizabeth Hagan opens her heart, describing with exquisite intimacy her excruciating feelings of biological failure, human disappointment, and divine abandonment. The reader looking for support while living through infertility will find a friend who understands, and the friend looking for ways to offer support will find answers in this warm and real account of the author's attempts to have the baby she so dearly wants." —Martha Spong, Executive Director, RevGalBlogPals, and Editor, *There's a Woman in the Pulpit*

"*Birthed* moves infertility out of the shadows where shame, guilt and discomfort have lodged it for far too long and teaches us that giving voice to our deepest fears and pain is the only way for hope and possibility to take root and flourish." —Edith Guffey, UCC Conference Minister, Kansas-Oklahoma

"Tired of the infertility taboo? Elizabeth lifts the veil with humor and raw emotion, guiding her reader through the journey of parenthood, interrupted." —J. Dana Trent, Author of *Saffron Cross: The Unlikely Story of How a Christian Minister Married a Hindu Monk*

"Elizabeth speaks with honesty and integrity about the excruciating reality of infertility. But somehow, in spite of such, she magically and miraculously weaves (and lives) a story of surprising beauty and blessing. *Birthed* is a true and tender book that offers its readers the priceless gifts of redemption and hope; she honors and models the enduring capacity of a woman's heart." —Ronna Detrick, *Transforming Women's Sacred Stories* blog

Birthed

FINDING **GRACE**
THROUGH
INFERTILITY

Elizabeth Hagan

Foreword by Amy K. Butler

CHALICE®
PRESS

ST. LOUIS, MISSOURI

Cover art and design: Jesse Turri

ChalicePress.com

Print: 9780827203112
EPUB: 9780827203129   EPDF: 9780827203136

Printed in the United States of Anerica

Contents

To Kevin: truly the best man I've ever known

Foreword

This story is your story.

It's mine too.

And that's the thing that's so alluring about the book you're holding in your hands, though you might not know it quite yet. At first glance I assumed this story was someone else's: a story of infertility, sad and painful, worthy of something like detached appreciation from those of us who have never spent a moment wondering whether or how we would become parents.

But once I began to read, the story gradually started to seem familiar.

Like every one of our stories, like my story, this one is filled with pain and decorated with beauty so intense that we can't believe it.

It takes a good amount of courage to voice the bleak desperation that is our shared human experience. We'd much prefer everyone saw the shiny veneer we so painstakingly cultivate in every way we can possibly muster. But you will read in this story an eloquent expression of pain, words to hang onto or appropriate to speak of your own.

Because we have to speak of the pain of human life so we can speak with any integrity of the joy we experience: the long-awaited realization of a lesson learned, the deepening of love, the assurance of the presence of God. The light and the darkness both color our humanity, and to speak of one without the other will never show us the landscape we so desperately long to see, the full story of each one of our broken and beautiful lives.

This book is about pain, but it's not just about pain. It's about love, too, and that's why it's your story. And mine. When I say love, of course, I'm not talking about a flowers and rainbows kind of love, or even a Harlequin romance love. In these pages you will read and remember what happens when love comes to find us curled up, alone, broken. And the times love pulls us close and holds us tight when the tears won't stop. And the times when love slaps us in the face and tells us it's time to pull ourselves together, get up off the floor, and do something, for God's sake.

In these pages you'll read about the flawed and miraculous love of a spouse, that person with a front seat to all the pain life throws our way, the person who gets splattered with all of the ugly and stubbornly refuses to give up his seat. And when you read this witness you'll recognize the beauty of that unique kind of love as you have experienced it.

And as you read, you'll recognize from your own life the love of friends, those people whose lives intersect our own lives, people who will not leave us to our own devices but instead walk through the darkness with us, holding our hands. These are the people who show up when nobody else wants to be there. They are the ones who pass the Kleenex, and they are the ones who tell us once and for all to get over the destructive fascination we have with our own pain. They cuss with us and at us, and sometimes they're the ones pouring the wine when all other options have been exhausted.

And when you read this story, you will recognize the unfailing love of God, in whichever way that has made itself known in your own life. While this one is a beautiful story, this is most certainly not the story of an over-achieving pilgrim whose exceptional holiness is rewarded with an extra dose of God's presence. No, like your story and mine, in this story you will recognize a wandering disciple naively demanding a rightful answer to the pain of human life. She doesn't know when she starts out that an answer isn't what she needs at all, that what she needs, in fact, is presence, a divine audience to her human outrage at the pain and injustice of it all. Just like you and me.

Read the beautiful, pain-laden words in this book. Read every single one, because when you do you will recognize yourself. And when you do you might find, as I did, that this story will help you grasp the courage you need to speak of your life in its fullness. You will know in the core of who you are that your experience is not a lonely aberrance.

And when you wake up to that awareness, like Elizabeth, you might just begin to recognize your own pain for the holy honor it represents, the rushing water that has smoothed your hard edges and the terrible chisel that has chipped away at everything superfluous and shaped you into who you were meant to be.

Whether you are a pastor, too, or whether you're the most faith-less person you know, whether you've agonized over IVF cycles or whether you've never spent a day in your life worrying about reproductive realities, I am telling you: you will find yourself in this story. Why?

Because this is not really a story about wanting to be a parent.

This is a story about becoming fully human.

This is a story about setting out to conquer the world and finding yourself on the side of the road, heart cracked wide open.

This is a story about finding a family, perhaps not in the places we thought at first, but instead in ways we'd never dreamed. It is a story of finding unlikely parents in our lives and learning to parent each other.

And this is certainly not a story about an inviolable faith that can withstand any pain and injustice that comes its way. It's rather a story about giving up control, finally, and letting God do the excruciatingly beautiful work of shaping us into the masterpieces we were created to be.

And which of us has never lived a story like this one?

Throughout my career as a pastor I've walked through the grief of infertility with so many couples. Infertility is a grief with nuances that are painfully familiar to those who have lived through the experience, and in the church in particular it is often a silent grief. How many in our congregations are sitting through baby dedications with their hearts breaking, suffering pregnancy loss that goes unnoticed, or reading baby shower announcements that innocently crack their hearts wide open? As we all have felt grief, we all know that a recognition of our grief by someone who has shared a similar experience can have a powerful healing affect. Those who have walked through the grief of infertility will surely feel that healing recognition when they read this book. It is a compelling story, but it is also a resource for those who are feeling this particular pain.

There are also many parts of the grief experience that are universal. While I myself have never personally gone through much of the journey Elizabeth invites us on in this beautiful book, there were moments in my reading that I felt the balm of recognition, that I felt my grief understood. Share this book with people who are living with infertility, and share this book with anyone who needs to know their experience of grief is shared. It is a healing gift.

Maybe you picked up this book because infertility is your particular grief. Or perhaps like me you opened this book to read a compelling memoir, a story that would capture your attention as any well-told story does. But if you're hoping to read with detached curiosity, I dare you to try. If you make it all the way to the end, you'll want to write and tell me that I was correct when I say you won't be able to do it. In one expression of this story or another, we all find ourselves. Curl up with this book and give it all the attention it will surely invite from your mind and your heart, and you will quickly find yourself in the story.

Because this is your story.

And it's mine too.

Amy Butler

Introduction

Infertility Wasn't Supposed to Happen to Me, but It Did
(and to a lot of other people too!)

You never expect bad things to happen to *you*. Well, maybe some bad things…but not *really* bad things, especially when it comes to your dream—your one big dream.

In my case, it was the dream of motherhood. In my dreaming, I never expected that I would have difficulty becoming pregnant. In my dreaming, I never expected I would undergo assisted reproductive procedures *nine* times. In my dreaming, I never expected I would write a book about my own infertility.

But then this worst-case scenario happened to me.

Call me naïve, but growing up in suburban, middle-class, Caucasian, conservative evangelical culture in Tennessee, I only heard traditional birth stories. I heard stories of mothers and fathers who wanted babies and had them. Was there any other way?

Though I'd overheard the words "test tube baby" on the nightly news that told of the first-ever child born through *in vitro* fertilization (conceived two years before my 1980 birth), I paid no attention. Why would I? My discreet mother rarely uttered the words for reproductive parts of the body or even the menstrual cycle, so "test tube babies" were well outside the realm of dinner conversation topics. And fertility doctors? What were they? No one I knew used them or talked about them.

I did have an acquaintance or two in my elementary school classes who shared "the secret" about their adoption while

1

twirling on the monkey bars at recess or over popcorn in the wee hours of the morning at slumber parties. I'd later muse with my mom, "Why are some kids adopted?" She'd answer me, "Some parents have babies they can't raise, and other parents who can't have children agree to raise someone else's child as their own."

Sounded simple enough, especially for me, a child raised by both biological parents. Adoption was something that happened to those outside my daily circle. If you'd asked me as an eight-year-old how I felt about my birth story, I would have told you, "I am glad to be like everybody else." It's good to be the kid without the playground secret. Yet, like most kids in my shoes, privately I always wondered what it felt like to be adopted.

And so I never knew about women who went through the effort of seeking medical intervention to have babies until I met Ashley. I was exposed to the harsh realities of baby-making during my first pastoral job. To earn extra money for school, I signed up to serve a small parish as a part-time pastor. My seminary assigned me to a rural North Carolina congregation with "Bud," who could have been my father, as my supervisor. I wasn't sure how well we'd get along—me, a young, ambitious "take on the world" seminary student, and him, a tall but round man, balding on the top, who enjoyed hunting and fishing in his free time. Pastor Bud's office was a tornado of NASCAR memorabilia and papers not in file folders. When I cried in that office my first day on the job, Bud responded by commenting, "I guess you have allergies?" I looked down at my red heels, trying to pull myself together. Despite our differences, the two of us learned a rhythm with each other. And, at this church, I first began to fall in love with the joys of being a pastor.

I loved preaching. I loved organizing service projects for the youth. I loved being invited into deep conversations in parishioners' homes. And I loved pulling together the children's time in the service every week, often getting my best ideas in the car on the way to church on Sunday morning. I was a planner, but could also easily weave lessons on the spot.

Every week Bud and I met to go over how we'd divide the congregational responsibilities. On one occasion our conversation lasted a bit longer. He knew I'd recently begun a new small group for younger couples. He told me about a sensitive issue facing two regular attenders, Ashley and Robert: "They're trying to have a baby and have been trying for some time."

"Oh, okay." I said, wondering whether this topic was worthy of such a formal sit-down conversation with my supervisor. Don't couples try to have children all the time? And, anyway, was this really any of my business or his?

I had not yet learned that some parishioners want to talk to their pastors about everything, including their sex lives.

Bud went on: "What you need to know is that they've tried everything. They've been through all kinds of treatment. They've miscarried a couple of times. I've prayed with them through the ups and downs of their process. I even made a visit to their home once to pray for them right after they had a procedure. They'd thought if I could pray over Ashley's stomach, it might help."

I slumped down into my chair. Apparently this was more serious than I thought. What a horrible strait to be in!

Bud continued, "I need you to know that they're really sensitive to the other couples in the class having babies. They so desperately want to be parents. But as hard as they try, it's just not coming easy to them. I don't understand, Elizabeth…"

I finished his sentence: "…why they don't just adopt?"

"I've tried to talk to them about adoption, but they'll have none of it. I don't understand. I've seen countless couples through the years not be able to have a kids, then adopt, and then soon be pregnant! It's just the way it seems to work."

I'd certainly heard this type of reasoning in hearsay conversations by now at my ripe old age of twenty-three, and I agreed with Bud. "Adoption is the *most* Christian way, you know," I said, proud to add to the conversation something we'd just discussed in my Christian Ethics class. Earlier in the week, I had sat at the feet of famed Christian ethicist Stanley Hauerwas, who told us repeatedly that adoption was the best choice for those in Christian community.

I'd written in my notes, "The church should be a place where abortion is not an option because the church looks after all God's children." In his lecture, Hauerwas seemed to look down on assisted reproductive technology, such as *in vitro* fertilization. If a couple couldn't have kids, they shouldn't idealize a biological family. They should just adopt.

As I continued to fill Bud in on the points I remembered from the lecture, my senior colleague looked pleased at what I was gleaning from my coursework at Duke Divinity School.

At the end of the conversation, I told him, "If I find a way to work it into one of my conversations with Ashley and Robert, I will. I'll try to encourage them to adopt."

What was I thinking?!

Thank heavens, the right opportunity for this conversation with Ashley and Robert never happened. I was not spiritually, ethically, or emotionally prepared to swim in such deep waters of pastoral relationship yet, or, for that matter, any relationship full of deep pain.

It had not yet happened to me, so I could not yet begin to understand a pain like this.

But when it did happen to me six years later, my grief did not come with "right," or more *spiritual,* solutions. Hauerwas's one-size-fits-all advice no longer resonated with me. I soon realized that until you've walked the path of an infertile woman or man, you don't have a clue what it feels like to want something so important so badly and not be able to have it. I realized that when you know in your heart that parenthood is your calling, there's nothing you won't try to bring a child into existence. And with time I realized that adoption is never the "solution" to making infertility all better—it's a choice of an altogether different discernment process.

But most of all, when it happened to my husband, Kevin, and me, I realized that infertility is still a taboo subject. It did not help to know that according to Resolve, the National Infertility Association, one in eight couples struggles to conceive naturally, which is approximately 12 percent of childbearing-aged women. We didn't want to be among the 12 percent. Who does?

I was overcome with shame, anger, and deep sadness. And I didn't want to talk about it!

Though the biblical narrative is full of stories of women who have struggled to conceive (Sarah, Hannah, and even Elizabeth), though great progress has been made in women's reproductive rights (Roe v. Wade, birth control accessibility, and so on), and even though some women in the public eye talk about their miscarriages without flinching (Courtney Cox, Tori Amos, and Brooke Shields), there is still something deeply emotional about being infertile that leaves women like me silent.

I am normally such an open person. At the time our infertility struggles began, I preached publically almost every Sunday. I had an internationally read blog in which I regularly addressed my faith struggles. Yet the one thing I couldn't discuss in any forum was my infertility. Why?

At home, my life felt like a big, gaping wound. My body wouldn't do what I expected it to do. And it wasn't like I didn't want kids. I liked kids. I loved kids. The church members I led often commented on how good I was with them. My undergraduate degree was in elementary education, after all! But as month after month passed and Kevin and I had no announcement to share, I felt shame. Something was wrong with me, and my deep fear was that everyone knew it.

I did not utter a word, because early on I had heard the stupid things people say when you put your deep fertility pain on the table. Things like, "Everything happens for a reason," or, "God makes everything perfect in his time." Or, even, "When God wants to send you your angel, God will." These platitudes offered no balm and actually made me feel worse.

Yet, there came a day when I could no longer be silent. As shameful as it was to take on the label of *infertile* given to me by my medical records, I could not be one of those infertiles who one day finally had a baby and simply forgot that this phase of her life had happened. I could not be one of those infertiles who whispered about her pain to her grandchildren. So I made a decision: I would speak. And I would speak even in the midst of an uncompleted story.

Because, what infertility gave me was a hope that I can only attribute to the divine mystery of things—a hope that would be renewed again and again, a hope that allows me to see both what is right in front of me and what is not yet. God birthed in me compassion not only for the Ashleys and Roberts of this world, but also for those who grieved in other ways.

I knew then that I'd write a birth story—though it wouldn't actually be about a baby.

Rather, it would be a story about my hell and my heaven. It would be a story about the depths of Good Friday, the certainty of being in the tomb on Saturday, and the joy that is resurrection on Sunday. It would be a story that readied me for motherhood by first making me a wife, a sister, and a daughter to others. It would be a story that healed parts of my heart that I didn't even know were broken. It would be a story that even now I wish hadn't happened to me, but it did.

Hi, my name is Pastor Elizabeth, and I am infertile. This is my story.

1

Adventures in Not Dating and Then…

In seventh grade after a lesson on sexual purity (the dramatic pep talk about "no sex before marriage" that was popular throughout evangelical youth group land), the youth pastor's wife took all the girls aside. During an all-night retreat, we spent hours on end hearing about the horrors of unprotected sex. Alternatives presented to us included praying for our future spouse and writing him a "These are my dreams for our marriage" letter. Though one girl in my grade interrupted, saying, "I don't want to be married," I knew I wasn't in this category. From the time I was a flower girl in my aunt's wedding at age five, I couldn't wait for my big day. I started praying and wrote that "Dear future husband…" note, and wrapped it up in a box with a bow. Seems a little extreme to me now, but according to a popular 1990's national campaign to which I signed my name, true love had to wait. It *always* had to wait.

Because good Christians waited, they got married young—*at least this was my experience.* I come from a long line of women who married young. My grandmothers married at age 20. My mom married at 23. My two older girl cousins married at 18 and 19. I assumed I'd follow such a timeline too. I believed I *was* a good Christian.

But enter a huge problem for my adolescent "True Love Waits" self: you eventually have to meet someone. And I wasn't the type to have lots of boys who were friends, much less boyfriends. Starting in middle school, boys + Elizabeth = pale face with no words coming out. Once, in my creative efforts to communicate with a boy I liked in eighth grade, I gave him my prayer journal, explaining to him via a note I passed his way in church, "This is how you can get to know me." You can imagine how long that relationship lasted.

But what I lacked in social skills, I made up for in God skills. I cared deeply about my faith and its practices and sacred texts. I memorized large chunks of scripture just for fun, starting in seventh grade at the invitation of a teacher. I read the Bible through twice in the seventh and eighth grades. *Really.* The whole thing (something I've not done since!). I organized "encouragement projects," such as randomly leaving candy bars in classmates' lockers when I knew they were stressed out or had a big basketball game coming up. I signed up for any sort of out-of-town service trip I could attend, even spending six weeks away from home as a sixteen-year-old teaching kids in inner-city Charleston, South Carolina. I knew that a big part of being a Christian meant following Jesus beyond your comfort zone, so I tried to be open to opportunities that came my way. I wanted my life to be about showing God's love.

But even with all that time I spent at church and on service projects, I also never wanted to be left out of major life milestones, like the prom. When I wasn't asked right away in junior year, I courageously asked the cutest boy that I thought might say yes. Ben played basketball, I managed the girls' team, so we saw each other often on the bus. We took many of the same AP classes. Why *wouldn't* he say yes? This was a bold move on my part, but I did *not* want to go alone.

Two weeks passed and I heard nothing from Ben. Four days before the prom, I sat in class doodling hearts around his name, still wondering why he had not responded to my invitation. I vowed to ask him again after our shared U.S. history class. I knew Ben was not dating anyone else. I was sure that he would go with me. My "let's get to the point" self wondered what the holdup was.

Then my worst nightmare materialized. Our teacher was chatting with us instead of presenting a lesson. When the teacher asked about my prom plans, I told him I didn't know. Soon it was my prospective date's turn to name his plans. The boy buried his head in his sweater, picking at the lint and fuzz with his mechanical pencil. He said nothing!

Suddenly the teacher put two and two together, realizing our potential match-up. "Now, isn't that interesting," he prodded. "I see a bright young lady over here who would be a good date for you." My face turned five shades of red. Luckily, the bell saved me.

Shy and humiliated, Ben said no. I went to the prom alone that year.

By the time I got to college, I knew dating success was crucial to my ultimate goal of finding a Christian partner extraordinaire. But my most memorable date in college came on a Sunday morning my freshman year. *Cue the sad music.* The boy and I attended church together, then ate stale sandwiches and chips from the cafeteria. In the end I wasn't even sure it was a date—maybe he'd just needed a ride?

So rather than focusing on boys in semesters to follow, I sought to graduate with honors from the education school. And I did. My hard work paid off when I landed my first job weeks before graduation, teaching fifth-grade kids in inner-city Birmingham, Alabama, the same town where I'd studied for four years.

However, while I loved teaching and being with children, it was really the bigger issues of community life that energized me. A couple months into teaching, I knew I wanted to lead communities of faith more than classrooms of kids. I had recently seen a woman leading a church for the first time, and in her I saw myself. I dreamed of leading the kind of church I'd never known in the strictness of my childhood—a church where the gifts of all people could be celebrated, where social justice was not an afterthought but the heartbeat of the community, where no one would be unwelcome no matter race, sexuality, or background. Passages of scripture that spoke of Jesus teaching us to "Love thy neighbor" and "Go into all the world and preach" fired me up. Maybe all those years of Bible study and journaling were telling me that I was made to lead.

At the same time, friends and mentors I met in college were nudging me toward seminary. "I think you would thrive there, Elizabeth," one of the campus ministers told me over and over again. I took the advice with both trepidation and excitement, and I leaped toward ministry as a potential vocation. Finally, in the fall of 2003, I landed on the steps of Duke Divinity School.

In the first few weeks at Duke, I sat wide-eyed in my first seminary classes beside amazing new colleagues on track toward becoming pastors. Of course, I still hoped I'd marry one day, but I rarely talked about it. I attended a seminary with one of the youngest student bodies in America. With most of my classmates in their early twenties and unmarried too, the campus felt like a safe space to focus on my career without concern for what was not yet. I finally found myself surrounded by people with callings and quirkiness just like me, who were also once Bible Drill champs and knew all the words to every Jars of Clay song.

However, in my first seminary internship, the same place I later met Ashley and Robert, church members seemed eager for me to marry. I just couldn't avoid the pressure. So many of them offered advice about finding "Mr. or Mrs. Right" such as, "When you aren't looking, he/she will come," and, "Do what you love and don't worry about meeting a partner, then he/she will come." I hated these clichés, but in my case they turned out to be true.

Out of nowhere came Kevin. Never in a million years would I have pegged myself to be with him, but we couldn't have been a more perfect match.

When people first meet Kevin, it's his larger-than-life presence that fills the room. He's tall with a warm smile, brown eyes, and hair thinning on top, and you never find him without a glass of tea in his hand from Starbucks. Relationally, he moves toward anyone he meets with a buoyant joy. He's quick to know when to respond to others with a laugh or a hug or a sympathetic

swear word during times of distress. He exudes wisdom that
often seems to come out of nowhere. And because of all of this,
most people want to be Kevin Hagan's friend.

We met after my second year at Duke, when I served as the
pastoral intern at the church he attended in Washington, D.C.
I had just started my dream summer of living and working
alongside a gifted female Baptist pastor. I'd never been so affirmed
in my calling by another woman, and I was in love both with
pastoring and with the vibrancy and diversity of the city of
Washington. Dating was far from my mind.

But then came Kevin. My first impression: he was a really
nice guy. He seemed very serious about his job and his Blackberry.
And he had a lot of beautiful friends. I'd only been in D.C. for
a few days when Kevin hosted a party at his apartment as a
going-away gesture for another member of the growing young
professionals group at the church. As I drank beer out of a red
plastic cup while he had a cocktail, with only a kitchen counter
between us, I quickly learned Kevin wasn't your typical churchy
type. Though raised in a Baptist church in the South like me,
he'd only recently come back to church after a decade away. He
liked the new church he'd recently joined, but it still bothered
him a little because it had a female senior pastor. He just wasn't
sure he believed in such a thing! Yet he was trying to wrap his
mind around the concept and was full of questions.

Still, I had a lot on my mind. Getting used to life in the city
for the first time took most of my brainpower. I couldn't imagine
that a guy like Kevin would ever pursue me!

Yet unbeknownst to me, after our first meeting Kevin was
already carefully mulling the pros and cons of asking me out.
"She's too pretty to be a pastor," Kevin told his best friend, Jeff,
one night. "Could I kiss her and not go to hell?" he mused.
"Would I be signing up for a life spent at church? Do I really
want church to be my life?"

As he tells the story now, the thoughts and worries over my
suspected holiness got the best of him; the summer came and

went, and he never made his move. I traveled back to North Carolina with a year of seminary studies left, and Kevin remained in D.C.

Then, in what seemed like a move from out of nowhere, Kevin decided to make one of his now-familiar "grand gestures." I received a phone call one Saturday afternoon from Kevin as he was "just driving through" the neighborhood in North Carolina where I was completing another church internship. Little did I know he had driven a hundred miles out of his way just for the chance of seeing me.

"Would you meet me for lunch tomorrow?" he asked. Quickly, I told him no. I already had plans to eat with a church member. It sounded juvenile and irresponsible to cancel a church lunch meeting for a date, but then again I'd always been a little too focused on what was right in front of me rather than seeing beyond. Did I like Kevin? I had no idea other than that he seemed like a decent man.

On the way to church the next morning, I mentioned the call to my mother (thank God), who floored me when she said, "Forget church, and call him right now."

Maybe I should listen to her? My policy at the time was never to say no to a first date, and I'd just broken it.

Over the course of the drive, I remembered all of the things Kevin and I had in common on the surface. He hailed from Georgia and I from Tennessee, so we are both Southerners. We both loved the D.C. church community; and, as an added bonus, he worked at Postal Service headquarters. (I always had a thing for the mail.) The more I thought about him, the more my curiosity was piqued. He already knew I was a pastor. I could be myself without having to bring it up awkwardly later. My excitement about a possible meet-up grew in those miles down N.C. I-40, so I called Kevin back right after hanging up with my mother, explaining that I could go to lunch with him after all.

He quickly changed his plans to accommodate, and we met at Logan's Roadhouse, the finest Sunday dining establishment in Goldsboro, North Carolina. After crunching some peanut shells on the floor, devouring buttery yeast rolls, and talking a lot about the D.C. faith community that was slowly changing both of our lives even though my connection to the church was now long distance, our relationship journey of becoming more than former church intern and church member began. As soon as lunch ended, I called Meredith, a new friend I had made while living in D.C., to share the big news. She knew Kevin too.

"I think I just went on a date with Kevin Hagan!" I exclaimed. Meredith squealed.

Suddenly my school schedule and my "work for God" seemed less important than when I would see Kevin next or when he would be calling at night. Though I was not sure how long the relationship with him would last, I was smitten. I kept worrying that a man as kind and put together as Kevin would soon lose interest in me. Still, Kevin kept surprising me. He was not like the guy I'd most recently dated in seminary, who believed a woman's place was a couple steps behind a man. Kevin always looked outward. By now his mind was warming up to female ministers and he talked about me with admiration in public. And most of all he listened well—the quality I had always wanted most in a husband.

Early on, Kevin recognized that I carry my emotions close to the surface. We'd dated less than six months and I was at his place for the weekend. Earlier in the day, I had received news that crumbled my vocational version of "happily ever after." I was not going to become the associate pastor at the church where I had previously interned for the summer. My beloved church could not afford another clergy staff member. My life felt ruined in a way that only a graduate school student in love looking for that first job can understand. Being a delayed processor, it took a couple of hours for the bad news to sink in.

Around 1:00 a.m., uncontrollable tears overtook me.

Kevin and his roommate, Rohan, both awoke, thinking that someone had broken into their condo. But when they arrived almost simultaneously in the back bedroom, peering down at me in a growing pile of tissues, they quickly knew this was no intruder.

Telling concerned Rohan to go back to bed, Kevin led me down the hall to his room. He found me a soft blanket and wrapped his arms around me. Through my hyperventilating shakes, he repeated, "It is going to be okay, honey. It's going to be okay."

I woke up late the next morning sure of one thing: Kevin Hagan was not afraid of my tears. He wasn't like others I'd befriended. He did not run away. He might just be a keeper after all.

As much as we loved each other, we had no easy path to marriage. There was the matter of navigating a long-distance relationship while I finished my time at Duke; months and months of uncertainty about where I would work after graduation; the question of whether I would ever find a job as a female Baptist pastor; and vocational transitions for both of us. Then, there was figuring out other changes like my moving into a position as a full-time associate pastor at a large congregation in Maryland and his moving into a position in corporate America, ending his ten-year run with the government.

Through all of these stress-filled moments, we discovered we worked well as a team. I helped Kevin see that life was not all about the car he drove or the home he hoped to own. He loved my sentimental gestures of support, like tracking down the original first season of *Saved by the Bell* (his favorite early nineties show) on DVD for his Easter basket. He loved that I adored his gang of friends and spent time shopping with female friends who had been like sisters to him. He loved that I caused him to think more carefully and theologically about his choices, leading him to consider, for example, why having American flags as decorations on his Christmas tree might not be the most spiritually appropriate way to celebrate Jesus' birth.

And Kevin opened me up to trust. Perhaps never did I love him more than when we were in the airport. Instead of going through the drama of never knowing where I'd put my I.D. and boarding pass, Kevin started volunteering to keep my things in his pocket, just in case. The amazing part was that I would let him. Though I had previously flown all around the world with great confidence as a woman on my own, I gave him control. He could hold my license and boarding pass because, truthfully, being in charge all the time stressed me out. I lost important papers and my keys all the time! With this understanding of our respective strengths and weaknesses, we became an unbeatable team. If we could travel well together, I knew we could do anything.

Around the house, we soon learned that I had an eye for details, such as remembering to do the laundry. Kevin taught me to enjoy the finer pleasures of life, such as a tasty, well-presented meal. I learned how to earn points at upscale hotel chains so that we could take low-cost vacations at a moment's notice.

By the fall of 2006, I began pestering Kevin about when he might pop *the* question. I couldn't wait to merge our lives together. And it needed to happen soon. As a pastor and a young woman (a combo under scrutiny already), I couldn't live with Kevin until we were married (though I would have loved to!). I felt uncomfortable kissing him goodbye in front of church people. And any chance of my getting pregnant before the wedding…that was completely out of the question! He understood our boundaries and kept saying, "It's coming. It's coming."

Then, when I least expected it—a typical Kevin move—he came up with another grand gesture.

Exhaustion ached in my bones after completing my first Advent marathon as full-time Rev. Elizabeth. I took the God-awful 6:00 a.m. flight out of town on Christmas morning, planning to spend the first part of the Christmas holidays at the Hagan compound, our affectionate term for the street where pretty much everyone in Kevin's family lives, except him.

As soon as I arrived in his South Georgia hometown, I took a nap. Kevin shook me awake five hours later (*Christmas for clergy is exhausting, y'all*), and he handed me a piece of leftover Christmas ham on a paper towel. We drove the golf cart the half-mile into the woods behind his parents' house to the pond house, which had been hand-built by his dad several years before. This sacred Hagan ground was made out of the bricks of the elementary school that both his parents had attended!

I looked forward to opening up presents and being alone in a room together unwatched. I needed a long kiss under the cabin's mistletoe. But Kevin envisioned something else.

Knowing how much I loved words and pictures of my favorite people, he arranged things so the last present I opened would be a computer-generated photo storybook called "The Journey of Us." This bound piece was a beautiful tribute to my love of language and his attention to detail. Page after page contained stories of our dating life and quotes from our friends about our relationship. I reached the last page. It was a picture of him dressed in his tux with a red bow tie. He was perched on one knee, and the caption above the picture read, "Will you marry me?" Before I had time to process the text, he opened the ring box before me.

I think I said, "Yes," pretty soon thereafter, but all Kevin remembers was my quick, ever-practical response of, "Is this ring insured?"

The three-carat ring with two yellow diamonds on each side of the central diamond was more beautiful than I could ever have anticipated. The previous summer, I'd been picking out rings I liked in his mother's J.C. Penney catalog with hopes he'd notice, but what he had chosen was a far superior gem.

"For me?" I asked. There was no one else in the room, but I just couldn't believe it.

On October 27, 2007, I became Mrs. Hagan. The "Mrs." in front of my name freaked me out a little when it finally happened. I'd always run best solo. But I quickly reminded myself not to be afraid. This was not just *any* guy. We would not have just *any* marriage. This was Kevin, my emotionally mature dream partner. We danced to the Jack Johnson hit

"Better Together" before cutting the cake. We were so much better together. So, I did not need to fear becoming his wife. Kevin didn't ask for me to leave my soul, my brain, or anything else about me at the altar.

In the middle of our reception, Kevin stopped the usual toasts and led everyone outside for a fireworks show, a solid fifteen minutes' worth of colorful bursts! Even more amazing, I learned that fireworks were illegal in the state of Georgia at that time. Yes, illegal! But Kevin's connections at the county courthouse helped him push through all the necessary paperwork to make it happen. When I asked him later why he had gone to all the trouble, he said, "You only get married once, and I wanted you to know how I felt about you."

My next surprise was our honeymoon. Here I was—a simple preacher girl, lover of all things thrifty and practical—on my way to Fiji. Anywhere out of the country would have been more than enough to wow me, but Kevin insisted on Fiji. Surprise fireworks and a trip to a tropical island literally on the other side of the world? This was all a part of life with Kevin. I was his beloved, and for his beloved, there was nothing he wouldn't do or try.

However, despite all the gestures of love, which I readily accepted, I was baffled and blind as to what having a man like this in my life meant. His love had not seeped into me as deeply as years of marriage would later allow, and no number of diamonds, vacations, or fireworks would change this. It would take time and something uncontrollable and rattling for me to begin to see things as they really were: Kevin loved me, really loved me.

It was now time to dream of making a baby.

2

Not a Good Time to Lose a Baby

During the week of Thanksgiving, and Kevin and I found ourselves in Florida for celebrations with my mother's side of the family. In the middle of a private conversation in our room about whether we'd go bowling or to the movies later that evening with the rest of the crew, I blurted out, "Kevin, I'm late."

I'd been off the pill for eight months. It was our second year of marriage. Being the planner of the two of us, I made sure we had sex on the optimal days every single month. But in the previous eight months, I'd always gotten my period exactly on the twenty-eighth day of my cycle. I realized "the time to be concerned that something could be wrong" neared (what doctors say to a woman in her twenties if she's tried unsuccessfully to get pregnant for a year), but I wasn't there yet. I had no previous problems or abnormal pain, so the overachiever in me knew our time was coming soon. How could it not? Women had sex and got pregnant all the time. The week before, I had received three baby announcements in the mail. One of them had come from a friend who had been married only three months!

"That kind of late? *Late* late?" Kevin replied as we sat facing each other in the downstairs guest room, each on a twin bed where we'd slept the night before.

"Well, all I know right now is that I should have gotten my period a week ago, and it hasn't come yet."

Our family was staying in a crammed three-bedroom condo with an ocean view, and in another small condo across the street. This was not the time or place to have this kind of conversation, with so many potential eavesdroppers lurking steps away in the adjoining kitchen, warming up plates of leftover turkey and green bean casserole.

"How do you feel? Do you feel ok?" Kevin asked with a hint of helplessness in his tone.

"Well, actually, now that you mention it, I have felt off recently: There have been bouts of nausea that come over me. They seem to be getting worse." I went on, "Today when we shopped at the mall, I felt completely overcome at some points with how bad I felt. But I didn't want to say anything then." I was gleeful but not ready to jump to any conclusions.

A couple of hours earlier, I had actually left the condo and walked down the street to the one place where cell phone reception was good enough to consult with "Dr. Google." I typed the words "pregnancy symptoms" and then hit "search." All of my symptoms could mean pregnancy or something else, Dr. Google offered. Bottom line: I needed to take a pregnancy test. I had never wanted to be pregnant so badly. I'd come a long way from my "True Love Waits" days.

I told Kevin all about this, and he agreed, "Something must be up."

"Yeah, but I don't want to take a pregnancy test here. We're sharing a bathroom with the whole house, for goodness sake! You know my mom—she'd be out-of-control happy if there was any chance at all I could be pregnant."

"I know! Let's just wait until we get home on Sunday." As the conversation ended, I tried to go back to not thinking about it. I was unsuccessful, of course.

"Could I really be pregnant?" I wondered. And wondered. And wondered.

Yes, I could. We'd been on vacation, after all, celebrating our second wedding anniversary. Taking a road trip through the American Southwest starting in Las Vegas, Kevin and I had had plenty of time to be together at just the right time without the distractions of work, friends, or anything else. How awesome to think that on this wonderful vacation full of time spent in such beautiful, rugged places such as Flagstaff, Arizona, and the

Grand Canyon, we may have gotten pregnant! Any children of ours needed a good "this is where you were conceived" story, though I knew they would roll their eyes at us later.

So, I walked the half mile to the grocery store down the street. I slipped out the door while Kevin was taking a nap.

Almost 30 minutes later, I was back with a pregnancy test in my hand. I stared at the box from the opening of the bag. Kevin was awake and found me standing paralyzed in the middle of the room, holding the bag.

"You couldn't resist, could you?"

"No."

Kevin smiled. He knew my instincts well. "Are you going to take it now?"

For several minutes I said nothing.

Then, "I think so, but I'm scared. But I've felt so bad. Not normal—almost out of my body… It is weird to imagine, but I might actually be pregnant."

Off to the bathroom I went, hiding the paper bag under my sweatshirt.

Minutes later, I emerged from the bathroom with the white stick covered underneath the brown bag. I propped the stick up on the bedroom dresser. I stared at it. I told Kevin to lock the door. He sat back down on the bed. He stared in unison. The directions on the side of the box said if there were two lines, pregnant. If there was only one, I was not.

I got one and a half.

Did this mean we had half a baby? Kevin and I resolved to take another test when we got back to our Northern Virginia home.

To allay my anxiety, I called Marie, my best friend from college. "Eventually you will know," she offered. "I've gotten one-and-a-half lines before too. The news could be bad or good. You'll just have to wait and see."

By Sunday night when we returned home, I was nearly two weeks late. Not getting my period seemed like a surefire sign, no matter what the pregnancy test said. I let myself go there, to that place of uncontainable internal joy. I sang a little louder in the shower.

Coincidentally, the following Wednesday I had already scheduled my yearly check-up with the OBGYN, a new doctor for me, who took the insurance that came with Kevin's job. The doctor would help, I was sure. I just had a few days to wait. *Sigh.*

Wednesday finally came. I took off the morning from the church that now called me senior pastor, knowing I'd work late into the night teaching a Bible Study.

Right away I filled out all the necessary paperwork and soon a young nurse called me back to the exam room. The nurse asked me a few questions, took my blood pressure, and told me to undress. I sat bare-backed to the wall, a paper gown covering only my front, waiting for the doctor to come into the room. As the door creaked open, the female doc and I made some quick impersonal introductions, and then the first question out of her mouth was as I expected: "When was the first day of your last period?"

"Um, six weeks ago," I said, and went on to describe my other symptoms too. "What do you think this means?"

"Well, that's interesting. Are you using protection during intercourse?"

"No. I haven't since last March," I boasted.

"Well, you could be six weeks pregnant. But I can go ahead and do your yearly exam regardless. A pap smear won't hurt your baby if you are pregnant."

Her words glowed with the kind of light that made my heart skip a beat. I thought to myself, "Did I really hear what I think she just said?" I couldn't believe it. *You could be pregnant. Your baby.* Right away I replayed these words over and over again in my mind.

The doc grabbed the door handle and offered: "Let me go see what your lab test said. I'll be right back."

Coming back into the room minutes later (which of course seemed like an eternity) with my name written in large letters at the top of her clipboard she announced, "You aren't showing pregnancy right now. But tests can sometimes be inconclusive. So this is what I want you to do. Come back every day to our office for blood work till you either start your period or we find hormone levels appropriate for pregnancy in our tests. By the end of the week, we'll get to the bottom of this. We'll know soon."

Okay, so we had a plan. Seemed strange, all this business of "you could be pregnant, you could not be," but I trusted the doctor. I'd do as she said. The next day I came back for blood work. Result: not pregnant. Then, again, and again.

Five days later my period came.

Devastation bled through me.

How could I be "kind of pregnant" before but not five days later? Calling the doctor later on that week for a consultation, I asked for an explanation. "You probably experienced an ectopic pregnancy," she explained. "It's when the egg gets fertilized but doesn't make it long enough to implant in the uterus. Not every pregnancy takes," she went on. "It's normal. Just keep trying. I bet you'll be pregnant again soon. Eat well. Take folic acid every day, and just have fun with it. Stress doesn't help."

I felt relieved to get a word of clarification, but at the same time confused. Why did *this* happen to me? I tried to remain positive. "Stress doesn't help," she'd said. If I could get pregnant once, I could get pregnant again!

My positivity only lasted for a couple of hours before tears overcame me. I'd never known a loss of hope like this before. I couldn't help but cry. A sense of intuition led me to believe that this moment was worth pausing for. But for how long? A precious life once lived in me. Now that life was gone. I recalled the scripture I'd once memorized from Job, which spoke of the Lord giving and the Lord taking away. I wasn't yet ready to enter into the conversation about how or why God allowed this to occur. I just knew I could not go back to work the following weekend as if nothing had happened. The whole world looked different. Our household was back to just Kevin + Elizabeth, not Kevin + Elizabeth + the hope of a baby on the way. But how could I voice how I felt?

Small talk with church members seemed so petty. Watching our favorite TV shows with whiny comedic characters felt so offensive. And the thought of having something meaningful to say from the pulpit on Sunday seemed impossible. And I didn't want to talk about it. Kevin, with curiosity, asked why. I told him I didn't like to talk until I had something to say. Growing up, when an adult asked me about my day, I almost always said, "Fine." And that was it. I got by with a lot of *fine*. Living with Kevin was my first experience of someone who didn't take one-word answers. I needed more time, though, to trust him with my uncensored thoughts.

Several friends came over for pizza and movies a couple of days later, as was a normal part of our life with neighborhood friends. My moodiness was still apparent in how snappy I was about whether or not we used paper plates. This led Kevin and me to face our first awkward conversation with some of our dearest couple friends. They wondered what was wrong with me.

Kevin spoke where I couldn't. "Elizabeth was pregnant, and then she was not."

Ohhhhhh.

What a buzz kill I was! No one knew what to say. No one rushed up to hug me. No one sent me a card later when they had more time to think about how devastating this must have been for us (*like I would have*). No one really did anything except make "I'm sorry" statements and eagerly change the subject.

Our silent journey of grief had begun.

Within days, the season of Advent—the four Sundays of preparatory waiting for the birth of Jesus began. For obvious reasons, Advent is not a particularly helpful time for women grieving about babies, especially if those women happen to be pastors. I loved Jesus, but I didn't want Jesus to be a baby right now, a baby about whom I had to say something profound! Yet there was no way around singing songs and reading liturgy about the expectation of pregnancy. And congregants, more than at any other time of the year, I believe, expect their pastors to be happy as they sing these songs. And Pastor Elizabeth was not happy! But, for the sake of the job I loved and the congregation that had embraced a twenty-eight-year-old as their pastor with gusto less than a year earlier, I tried my best. I preached as well as I could. I would not fail at Advent season #1!

Beginning a new tradition, I offered a short evening vesper service for each of the four Wednesday nights in December. Going along with the traditional words of Advent—*hope, peace, joy,* and *love*—each week we focused our discussion on a new word. First up: *hope*. "Hope week" came four days after our devastating news. One of our corporate prayers in the book we followed asked us to reconsider what we were hoping for in the coming year and whether or not we were allowing God to be a part of our hopes.

I did not dare say my hope aloud: "I want to have a baby." However, I said it to God over and over during each moment of the silence we observed at the end of the service.

Several days later, we sang, "Come, Thou Long Expected Jesus" as we lit the Advent candles. I wondered how long Kevin and I would have to wait for another pregnancy. Another month? Six months? A year? We were ready. Wasn't God ready to bless us?

Oh, Jesus, all I want for Christmas is two lines on stick!

Instead, I got a lot of sweaters.

Two months passed. My thirtieth birthday neared. Of course I would be pregnant by thirty! What couple in love like us wasn't?

One morning, much to my glee, I started to feel sick, just like at Thanksgiving. Best of all, my period was late too. My body hurt. Kitchen smells that used to be my favorites, such as bananas and cheese, now repulsed me. Something was up, but this was no time for an obsession about all of this. Houseguests were on their way to visit us—my friend Marie and her husband, Bob, from Tennessee.

Ever since Marie and I became best friends in college, it seemed that she was the one person I could depend on more than anyone. When my beloved maternal grandmother died, Marie was at the funeral and took me out for beer and pizza afterward. When no one else came to visit me my first year of seminary, Marie did. When Kevin and I started to date more seriously, the first person I wanted him to talk to on the phone was Marie.

When Marie and Bob bought their plane tickets for D.C., Marie and I discussed our sightseeing adventures at length. The two of them had never spent much time in the city, so the possibilities were limitless. I couldn't wait to show them around.

Their plane landed and I met them in baggage claim, but the same fake smile came over my face. I wanted to put the troubles of the past couple of months behind me. I wanted to hope for a better future (perhaps one already underway?) And, most of all, I wanted to enjoy the specialness of this visit of dear friends.

However, in the hours to come, as much as I tried to enjoy the fun that these houseguests offered, I was in my own world. All I could think about on the Metro, as we toured museums, and as we feasted on yummy food in Chinatown was whether my period was going to come or not, when the last time I felt nauseated was, and when I might get the courage to take a pregnancy test. I was so afraid of another loss.

Kevin loves company, so he became social-chair-in-chief, managing all the details that came with hospitality: making reservations, picking up extra food, and driving the four of us around when we went out. This was great considering I couldn't get focused enough to make a single decision.

Sunday came—my birthday, my thirtieth birthday. How stupid to think that preaching on such an emotionally charged day was a good idea! But in my second year of full-time solo pastoring, self-care was not at the top of my list. Rather, proving myself was! I was *the* pastor of a Baptist church. My appointment to this position one year earlier had made headlines in my denomination. At the time, few women my age got this kind of opportunity. I didn't want to screw it up. Missing one Sunday would screw it up. So I would be there, birthday or no birthday. At least Marie would hear me preach!

As was my custom, I headed toward church a little before eight. Marie volunteered to go with me, leaving our husbands at home to finish getting ready. It was the first time that she and I had spent much time alone the entire weekend. We buckled our seatbelts in my small sedan and were off on the twenty-mile commute.

Marie looked dressed for such a monumental occasion: going to see her best friend's church for the first time. Her floral printed wrap-around dress with black hose and black high heels suited her blonde hair in an up-do. *Man, she looked so beautiful!* In contrast, tear stains covered my gray blouse and black knee-length skirt, I looked like I was going to a funeral. A run was in the process of forming in my hose around my big toe. I hoped I could make it all day without it getting worse. And my *hair*—let's not talk about how it frizzed it was! Yet, right away, Marie noticed the mood beneath my outfit.

"What's wrong?" My answer came in sobs (making her fear for her life, I'm sure, as we flew down the interstate).

"I started spotting this morning. And I haven't been nauseated for over twenty hours."

Trying to lighten the mood, she offered, "Really, twenty hours? You've being counting that precisely?" But this was not the time for jokes. My heart quivered in anticipation of all that I believed would come.

Marie got the point, and pulled out Starbucks napkins from the glove compartment of my car. She handed me several as I tried to wipe away my tears.

"Well, you don't know until you know. Just wait and see. Spotting isn't always bad."

I knew this pain of mine hit close to hers—she and Bob had been trying to get pregnant for over a year. I saw Marie's strength, but I also expected more from her. Why was she not crying too? Previously, Marie's advice had always worked wonders to calm me down. But that day no relief came. My car filled with silence for the rest of the drive. I wished our similar sadness could bond us, but neither of us knew what to say.

In the hours that followed, I stumbled through my sermon on the deadly sin of anger for our special Lenten series, losing my place several times. As much as I wanted to impress Marie with how much better I was preaching, I was just happy when the sermon was over so I could sit down. I said the benediction and dismissed everyone to go downstairs to enjoy our weekly potluck after worship. I felt silly for having expectations, but I was sure there would be a cake. There wasn't. I needed to eat my own words I'd just preached on anger as I peered over the dessert table. Someone told me that since we'd just had one for my first anniversary I didn't need another one. *Really?* Most of all, I felt so stupid for giving the church emotional control over my birthday. Oh, and we weren't done yet. Next came church council!

I ran to my upstairs office on the third floor of the building to grab my calendar and a few notes before walking down the hall, where a potentially contentious gathering awaited me. We'd make in the next hour or two what I thought were important decisions about the future of the church and its leadership.

Would we pay a new nursery worker, or would we find more church volunteers for Sunday school? Would we send out a memo to the other renters in the building about the missing locks on the paper towel closet, or would we ignore the fact that some renters seemed to be stealing them? Would we merge the worship committee with the hospitality committee, or would we leave them as separate entities in the by-laws? Such were the makings of what it took to manage life together in this community, the community that I was in charge of leading.

Making one last stop in the bathroom in between my office and the meeting room, I shut the door, hoping to put my "I'm a professional" face on. I decided to go into the bathroom stall as well. It was going to be a long meeting. The printed agenda was already two pages long, and that was only if additional items weren't added to it (*and they usually were!*).

Yet as I pulled down my pants, I saw the horror: my period. Bleeding over two weeks late again, bleeding harder than I'd ever experienced in any other cycle. A particular dream was over. A child was lost. My child. My hopes, my planning (that I'd be popping out a baby by 2011!), my sharing the good news with friends—these dreams were all crushed as I sat alone on the toilet in the women's bathroom. I could get pregnant again. Or could I? Though I heard several church council members inquiring in the hallway outside the door, "Where is Elizabeth? Where is the pastor? We need to start the meeting now," I just sat there. I couldn't move. I felt the pain throb all over.

Did anything else really matter in that moment? Did my pain matter to my church? I wanted it to. But I didn't think it did. What they needed from me was strength and what I defined as "professionalism."

So, as much as I wanted to wail and wail and tell the whole world what had happened to me again, I bit my tongue. I shut up my tears. I found a tampon under the sink—protection I'd hoped I would not be using again for many months—and washed my hands. I unlocked the door, gulped in a breath of air, and robotically moved myself down the hall toward the church council.

"Let's have a prayer before we begin, shall we?"

3

The St. Michaels Covenant

Two years into our married life, I thought Kevin and I had a strong marriage, at least better than most. We looked forward to togetherness after work each night. We talked about what bothered us more than we didn't. We each smiled when the other walked into a room. We proclaimed, "I love you!" before ending any phone conversation or before drifting off to sleep at night. *Well, mostly. Truth be told, if anyone held back affection after an argument, it was me.*

When our baby-making woes began, I wanted to protest that it was *my* body getting periods, it was *my* body crying for the loss that flowed through me, it was *my* friends whose pregnant bodies began to show new life in ways that mine did not, and it was *my* life that seemed to grow more disconnected to the core of what it meant to be a woman. Not *his*. So why should I talk to *him*? After experiencing so many lost hopes already, every night when Kevin said it was time for bed, I'd run up the stairs before he could get there and make myself a pallet of blankets on the fuzzy rug at the foot of our bed. I'd lie down and sometimes pretend to be asleep before he'd have time to object to my sleeping position. Though seemingly soft at first with all the blankets under me, the hard wood below soon began to push its way up into my spine. Every bone in my body ached those nights. But I didn't care. I liked it. This space on the floor came to symbolize how much I ached. The floor felt as I did inside: hard and lonely. If I uttered a word of my thoughts to our gang of friends, they'd say, "You'll be pregnant soon," with cheerful smiles. But, at this point, I was worried about making it to the next day.

Kevin hated my sleeping on the floor (*of course*). He'd do everything he could to lure me back: "Honey, why don't you come back to bed? Snuggle with me? It's really nice up here." But his words fell on deaf ears. I didn't know how to be with someone while I was in so much pain.

For Kevin, my sleeping habits became the thing he could not explain away with his "let's be positive about everything" attitude. As he watched me curl up on the rug night after night, some of his dreaming died too. I know he wondered when his wife would be normal again. I know he missed my laugh and how his jokes used to resurrect me from my sullenness.

On those occasions when I courageously tried climbing back into our actual bed, Kevin cheered me along. "See, isn't it more comfortable up here? Why don't you sleep here tonight?" he'd say. Then, since he regularly fell asleep faster than me, I'd crawl back out onto the floor when I sensed he would not notice. Just like that, my routine began all over again.

One Thursday afternoon, a day off for me, I was trying to eat but soon realized I was only staring at a soggy mountain of cereal mush and milk in the bowl. As tears flowed down my cheeks, my hands grasped their way to a Bible. From its pages, Psalm 13 found me. Two words of the psalm captured me: "How long?" I knew they were mine. My pain was leaking out of any crack it could. My litany writing began, and I posted it on my blog when I finished:

> *How long, O LORD? Will you forget me forever? How long will you hide your face from me?*

> When will this pain quit drowning me in the sea? I'm fully aware that life is unkind. This fact is for sure, but why rub it in, God?

> *How long will my enemy triumph over me?*

> I thought I was strong. I thought I could pretend. I thought I could be different from all the rest. I thought I could overcome. But, alas, the uninvited one comes and stays long past time. There is nothing I can do to evict

him. In fact, the guest announces, "I've made a home under your roof for an indefinite stay."

Look on me and answer, O LORD my God. Give light to my eyes, or I will sleep in death; my enemy will say, "I have overcome him," and my foes will rejoice when I fall.

There has to be something, anything, more than the brokenness of this guest. "Leave now, please," I demand. "NOW!" I yell. I long for the new.

But I trust in your unfailing love; my heart rejoices in your salvation.

I say, "I'm still alive. I'm putting one foot in front of the other. This must be something." And the light smiles.

After posting the entry, I received two concerned emails from a friend and a church member, "What's going on with you? Are you all right? I read your blog." I explained the concern away. It's a pastor's trick, after all, to claim your pain in the stories of "someone you know." And no one questioned that this was someone's else pain. Yet my soul was not well. My marriage was not well. I couldn't stay sleeping on the floor forever. Pastor Elizabeth wanted to challenge God to a wrestling match. My blog attempted the challenge.

Amidst all the grief, though, my friendship with Meredith felt like the one balm. Meredith's presence brought big spoonfuls of nurture into my life. Over long lunches after shopping trips we'd often talk about beautiful writing and exchange our favorite books. Or we'd find ourselves in a profound conversation in which, before we knew it, one if not both of us would tear up. In her, I gained the big sister I'd never had—the kind you actually really like and can't wait to call when something good or bad happens. The kind that you know wants your success more than her own. As we became closer, I told Meredith about our baby-making woes. No one else knew beside Marie. And it was to Meredith that I first voiced the frustrations with the lack of patient care from the OB/GYN I had seen months before. She told me over and over, "You deserve the best care. Fight for it."

Meredith's two kids were already in elementary school, and she seemed eager for me to experience motherhood too. "You are going to be a terrific mother," she told me over and over again. Meredith's goal-driven personality began to manage my dreams of motherhood. Regularly she'd ask me where I was in my cycle and whether I thought I could be pregnant "this month." I loved that she cared so much to ask. We'd make sex jokes with each other, as only girlfriends can do when talking about their husbands.

Then, one day when we were shopping for shoes, she urged more specifically, "Why don't you try another OB to get checked out? It wouldn't hurt to find out what's been going on these past couple of months, would it?"

I power walked toward the tennis shoe aisle, hoping she'd change the subject, but she didn't.

Staring at me with her dark brown eyes fixated on me, with her hands on her hips, she offered: "Maybe a new OB could run some tests and even give you a drug or two to speed things up."

Of course I was interested in her idea, but the thought of actually admitting I needed medical help overwhelmed me. Yet the more I thought about it, Meredith's suggestion gave me something to do. Like her, people called me "a woman of action." I knew how to get things done. So why was this "problem" in my life any different?

Thanks to Yelp and some advice from our family doctor, I called a new OB and made an appointment. I would re-start the conversation with her about my baby dreams. The doc's timely, perky response to my initial email encouraged me. Maybe Meredith was onto something. The right medical help could make the situation better!

The day of my appointment came. Kevin's work took him out of town that week, so I planned to go alone. I tried to convince myself that it was no big deal that Kevin couldn't come. But when I casually mentioned it to Meredith, before I realized it, I was holding a damp phone screen in my hands. My fears started spilling out. Meredith heard what I most needed: a friend. "I'll be there. Tell me when."

Quickly, I fought back: "You don't have to. Tuesday. I know you are busy." But what I really meant was, "Yes, please, please, please come. I'm so scared!" (*Maybe I needed to work on saying what I really felt. But this would be for later*).

By changing her after-school childcare plans, Meredith timed her arrival to meet me in the parking garage so we could walk in together. In a matter of seconds, new understanding flooded me as to why parishioners requested I go with them to the doctor. Being in a waiting room alone is scary stuff, especially with dreams of life on the line!

Meredith sat beside me in her black pants, trendy high heeled boots, and red sweater; funky rings on her fingers. She would have held my hand if I had wanted her to, but this visit wasn't that scary *yet*. As the nurse called my name, Meredith did not ask, but rather told me she was coming with me. "You shut down and don't listen when you are nervous. This is why I am here. I'm going to take notes for you and Kevin on everything the doctor says."

I probably rolled my eyes a little. But she went on: "Remember the first time we met? I want the doctor to like you."

Meredith spoke the truth. She was right. I had warmed up to her slowly. When we first met, introduced by coworkers, she talked a lot, and I said little. It's funny now that we became friends because Meredith wasn't sure she had the patience for my noticeable Southern accent. Luckily, we met up again.

The doc asked the nurse to draw some blood, took down my medical history, and reassured me that getting pregnant soon could happen. "Be patient," she offered. I still had not gotten my period this month. "I'm one week late," I offered her. That was enough to make us all hope. The doc said that someone from her practice would call back by Thursday afternoon with the results of the blood test. "We'll get to the bottom of what is going on with you soon!" It wasn't what I wanted to hear, but then I never boasted of having the spiritual gift of patience.

Meredith insisted we visit a pharmacy downstairs before we left the building. I needed the best pre-natal vitamins and folic acid supplements, she said. How could I argue with that?

She'd had two babies. I'd follow her lead. Thanks to Meredith and the new doctor's positive vibes, I started believing again. Maybe—just maybe—now was *my* time. Eventually, I would get pregnant. Most people did!

Beginning at noon on Thursday, I waited by the phone, since the nurse said this was the earliest she might ring me. I felt unable to do much of anything else on my "work-from-home day." When the call did come at 3:47 p.m., the nurse said simply, "Mrs. Hagan, you aren't pregnant." I stopped listening after that.

I fell right away to the living room floor rug and didn't move for hours. Though I was only a week late, and maybe my mind shouldn't have gone there, all that mattered is that it had. Another case of "I could have been pregnant and now I was not" consumed me. Kevin came home an hour after I'd texted him the news. He found me in the fetal position. But, then, Kevin reminded me how I'd committed to preach at a local seminary's chapel service that evening at seven. Pastor Elizabeth was not done with the day! *How could this be?* Thank goodness I'd already printed my sermon and laid out my robe and Bible next to the door. Now, if only I could get my body moving in that direction and stop the flood coursing down my cheeks.

Kevin walked upstairs with me to our bedroom. He opened the closet door and guided me toward a clean and proper church outfit. He unbuttoned a black polka dotted dress which fell to my knees and put it over my head while I just stood there. He invited me to put on my tan pantyhose and some black Mary Jane flats he dug out of my closet. "I would do it for you, but it's your job, honey," he said pointing to my hose. I followed his instructions. We made our way to the car and drove to the school. Kevin reminded me that sobbing in front a big crowd was not a good idea. Of course, I should have canceled, but Pastor Elizabeth did not say no to duty. The seminary president was a friend of our church. So I preached. I read the words on my 8½ by 11 white sheets of paper. I said amen and sat down. Did my sermon that night change anyone's life? Probably not. But I didn't cry until we got to the car. Huge win!

We picked up Thai food on the way home. I could only eat a few bites as I sat crossed-legged on the couch, dressed again in my fuzzy pajamas.

Kevin and I usually headed for bed around eleven. We'd wind down the day by watching the nightly news recap on CNN. But when 11:00 p.m. came on this Thursday night, restless energy flowed through my body like I'd never known. I could not lie beside Kevin on the couch. I could not sit still at all. Instead, I paced out figure eights around the main floor of our tiny townhouse, saying things like, "We should buy all white furniture if we aren't going to have kids. Isn't that what adults without kids do? And we should buy pointy coffee tables too. And we should go to the wine store next week. We should make a point of drinking lots of red wine. Lots of it. And if we spill it on our new white couch, who cares?"

Though Kevin would laugh about the ridiculousness of this night later, at the time (*White couches? Pointy coffee tables?*), my proclamations were serious. And my tirades had only just begun.

As I ran up and down the steps to our bedroom, I offered, "I know why people kill themselves. It's because of the pain. The pain is so deep. You want to get rid of the pain. You kill yourself to get rid of the pain."

Saint of God Kevin finally got the wine glass out of my hand. He dismissed me from the living room. He ordered me to bed, no questions asked. And in my drunken state, I passed out in bed.

Of course, I woke to a throbbing headache as daylight came through the window above our bed. The first thing I saw was Kevin standing over me rubbing my forearm saying, "Rise and shine." Orienting myself, I picked up my glasses from the floor and glanced at the alarm clock across the room. It read 9:30 a.m. I realized then that, in all my self-pity, I'd forgotten about Kevin's weekend trip—a trip for which he was due to leave in an hour.

"What are you doing here? Why aren't you at the airport?" Kevin and his best pals had planned this weekend away for months. One of them was to get married in a couple of weeks, so they were going to meet up in Vegas. I knew he'd been looking forward to this trip for a long time!

But, as I rubbed my eyes I could sense Kevin's seriousness: "I want you to come downstairs so we can talk." He handed me two Advil.

Thinking his flight was already delayed (*this would be the only reason Kevin would still be at home*), I climbed out of bed, dreading the day ahead. I knew task number one included editing the bulletin for Sunday's worship guide before the office administrator called to beg for it at 10:15. Maybe then I'd crash at Meredith's house?

I plopped down on the other side of the couch from Kevin. He just came out with it: "Elizabeth, I am worried about you."

"Well, duh. I'm worried too. But what does that matter to you?"

"It matters *a lot* to me."

And without taking a breath he laid out the plan: "I've spoken with Meredith this morning, and this is what we decided. I'm not going to Vegas, and you're taking a Sunday off."

"What!? You *have* to go to Vegas. I can't take you away from your friends! And I most certainly can't take the Sunday off! For what reason do I *deserve* time off?"

"You matter to me, Elizabeth. You're more important than this trip. I've already called Jeff (Kevin's best friend). He understands. Our marriage is more important than the guys, and it's more important than your church. Meredith is calling around with names I gave her. We will find you a fill-in preacher. Calls have already been made."

Even as I protested, Kevin was resolute. He wanted to be with me. He *needed* to be with me, he repeated. He was not going to Vegas. I stood dumbfounded and cross-armed in the middle of the living room. But Kevin wasn't finished. He called the chair of the church council. I listened in as he told her vaguely why I needed some unexpected time off. He asked her not to tell the congregation any bit of it, as he knew I would want this privacy. *Right on, Kevin.* So, like it or not, I would not be leading Sunday's service. I would be with Kevin at somewhere TBD. We were about to go away together even though we'd just had our regularly scheduled "fun Saturday off" seven days before.

Using Kevin's gift of quick Internet research, we settled on a two-night stay at a bed and breakfast in the small coastal town of St. Michaels, Maryland, about an hour and a half from our home in Northern Virginia. While packing, I kept asking him, "Are you *sure* you want to spend the weekend with me?" Sniff. Sniff. "I'm so sorry about your boys' trip. I've messed this all up."

But with each piece of clothing I tucked into my Vera Bradley weekend bag, I slowly settled into the idea. Maybe this wouldn't be so bad. Kevin and I really did need some time together. My optimism lasted only until we got into the car. A panic attack came on as we crossed the state line. Barely able to breathe, I grabbed a leftover grocery bag from under the seat and began panting into it. Did Kevin really know what he was getting into, being with me when I was such a wreck? I couldn't imagine him enjoying spending a weekend with me like this— sobbing, emotional, and unpredictable.

"Why are you kidnapping me?" I kept repeating as we cruised down Highway 50 toward the coast. "I know you are going to hate me by Sunday! Are you sure you want to do this?"

At first Kevin was calm: "Of course my dear. I want to be with you." But I simply could not compute how this could be true. So I repeated my question over and over, to the frustration of my calm-as-a-cucumber guy.

His tone soon became more forceful: "I love you. You have to let me be with you in this. You have to. We aren't going to make it otherwise."

Wow… Our marriage depends on this weekend? That got my attention. This was a side of Kevin I'd never seen before. Maybe it had always been there. But this new Kevin—the "I want you in all your drama. I am going to fight for you no matter what" Kevin—radiated brilliantly before my eyes. I finally heard him. Was this wonderful man really *my* husband? Could I trust him with not just my loud crying, but the loneliness in grief that I'd never spoken about with anyone? I had a weekend to find out.

I took a deep breath.

Though neither one of us had ever been cutesy, grandma's-house-bed-and-breakfast kind of people, the "Inn by the Sea" proved the perfect location. Our room's pink floral wallpaper invited us into hibernation together, as if we were at the home of an old beloved aunt.

We unloaded our luggage along with the bottle of wine we'd purchased at the liquor store on the way in. I couldn't believe that after last night he'd let me near another bottle of wine, but, hey, he was being kind. We found our way outside to some white plastic patio chairs facing the bay. I grabbed an extra blanket from the top shelf of the closet to cover up in the night breeze. A couple of glasses of Merlot later, I opened up to Kevin for the first time in a long time. I offered up the big questions:

"What if I can't give you a baby... Will you leave me?"

"What if we can never have kids?"

"What if we end up being the only childless couple among all our friends?"

"What if this whole process makes me lose my faith and I can't pastor anymore?"

Though he had suspected that my thoughts dwelled in these dark places, he had never known the specifics. As I kept talking, he listened without judgment. I went on for over an hour. And in response, Kevin told me about a difficult year in his life we'd never talked much about—his thirtieth year, full of so much pain: diagnosed with a cancerous tumor below the skin of his right arm, a serious management crisis at work, and then the diagnoses of a rare hip condition requiring surgery and a recovery of three months on crutches and another year and a half with a walking cane. He too had faced all of the questions of, "What if?" and, "Why me, God?" and knew how lonely suffering can be.

"But this is what I know, Elizabeth: we all go through hard stuff. We do. And when we surround ourselves with people who love us, we get through it."

As my head hit the pillow several hours later, exhausted, I thought for the first time that maybe we could survive this new label of "infertile" hanging over our marriage. We could get through this if we talked honestly, like we'd done tonight.

In the morning, without hurrying, we indulged ourselves

on freshly made omelets and scones in the inn's dining room. Neither of us remembered the last time we'd shared a Saturday together without an agenda for accomplishing activities. We then decided that our work for the rest of the day involved lying in the hammock strung between two oak trees overlooking the sea. We feasted for dinner at a lovely little pub in town.

I largely ignored my phone all weekend. But I glanced at it on Sunday morning and saw a text from Meredith. She wondered how we were doing. I'm sure she didn't expect a text back, but I was glad to hear from someone outside of this bubble. I told her about the porch chat and the day in the hammock.

Then she wrote back: "Why don't you make a list of what you and Kevin need from each other to stay in this process and what you promise to do for each other before coming home?"

My first thought was, "She's so bossy!" My second was, "What a wise idea!"

Though seemingly silly, like a game I would make up on the spot for a couple coming to me in crisis, I told Kevin about it. We were up for trying anything.

The hammock seemed like the best place for such serious daytime conversation, so back to our little cocoon we went. On the back of a napkin we'd saved from the previous night's dinner, we wrote our promises to one another, promises to love each other no matter what, promises to go to doctors' appointments together, and promises to ask for help when we needed it. Such words became the guiding document of hope we called the St. Michaels Covenant.

On our way out of town, we stopped at St. Michaels Winery for a wine tasting around the time I'd normally be leading worship. Several jokes about communion wine ensued, and Kevin and I decided to take a bottle or two home with us. Then, Kevin piped up with an idea: "Why don't we buy one really special bottle of wine from here and hold on to it until our baby-making project is complete?"

"Like the bottle of wine from California that you opened the night we married?"

"Yeah, like that… Our St. Michaels wine can be our special thing, saving it for one amazing celebration when Kevin Jr. comes into the world!"

"Or, Elizabeth II," I added.

How far we'd come just with a little time to exist as a couple again…

We both smiled.

Kevin really loved me. It was a miracle that I finally knew it. Next would come my living like he did.

4

I Love You and Won't Let You Go

By late September of 2010, Kevin and I had been on our trying-to-have-a-baby adventure for a year and a half. The St. Michaels road trip seemed light years ago, as the normality of daily life accosted us. Sometimes, we thought the worst: "What if infertility never ends? What if we are *that* couple that the doctors couldn't help? What if we never have kids?" But meaningful work saved us from these dark places. Kevin poured himself into his position as a Chief Operations Officer. He helped to resurrect a nonprofit whose mission centered upon putting excess products from corporations into the hands of nonprofits who needed the goods. His colleagues leaned on him for vision and his excellent administrative skills. The challenge of doing business in the nonprofit world spurred him on.

In my congregation, I helped the leaders dream about how an ecumenically minded Baptist church in Northern Virginia could have a strong voice. I preached weekly, visited the sick, and counseled the frustrated. Somebody was always in crisis, and, when they called, I was there. Even with my own pain weighing heavy on my heart, I loved being a pastor. The congregation seemed to love me too. Our numbers on Sunday morning increased. Soon my employment status moved from three-quarters-time to full-time. While it was not the success either of us most wanted, professional achievement felt like a balm to our baby-making woes. We didn't suck at *everything*, thankfully.

Back on the baby front, Meredith never left our side. She continued to come to OB appointments with me when she could make arrangements for her kids to be elsewhere. On the afternoon of one particularly important test, she actually stopped by the hospital on her lunch break to see if my fallopian tubes were open and fully functional (and they were!). She checked in regularly with Kevin and me on her way home from work, wondering how we were coping. She always ended the conversations we shared by asking, "What's the next step?" Our love for this sister ran deep.

Once all the tests concluded, the only real problem discovered by our now-contracted fertility specialist was low sperm quality. I could have the best eggs and uterus in the world, but without quality sperm, natural pregnancy would prove very difficult. The doctor invited us to consider trying *in vitro* fertilization (IVF). *Enter three big scary letters into the conversation.* He said the lab could help us choose the best sperm and achieve our goal of pregnancy faster. It wasn't that we couldn't get pregnant and stay pregnant on our own, but the chances, the doctor admitted, were slim.

For weeks we pondered those letters—I, V, and F. But then, at our follow-up appointment, we declared that if IVF was what we needed to do, then we would do it. After overcoming the initial shock, neither of us thought twice about this decision. We had a medical problem; someone was offering us a medical solution; why would we not seek medical help? Though some Christians might have told us that IVF is "immoral" or "playing God," such thoughts never crossed our minds. *Never.* Sure, we gave over the miracle of conception to a lab, but who said that God couldn't bring life to our family through a petri dish? We both believed in the miracles of modern medicine. Though I'd had limited exposure to couples attempting IVF, who said it wasn't right for our family at our moment of need? Maybe it was God's way of blessing our family. We'd never know if we didn't try. Though our insurance didn't cover such a procedure, the tax refund check we'd gotten earlier in the year made us confident we'd be okay financially. In fact, the presence of this windfall seemed further confirmation this was the right track for us.

The process began with signing necessary contracts with the fertility clinic (all twenty pages of them!). We checked the box on the first page choosing natural cycle IVF as our procedure, just as the doctor recommended. Unlike regular IVF, where the goal is to harvest lots of eggs in one cycle through daily injections of hormone shots, natural cycle IVF included no shots.

On just the right day of the month, one egg—the one I'd produce naturally—would be extracted from me while I was under localized anesthesia. Then, the lab would select the best of Kevin's sperm and carefully insert it into the egg. We would then wait and hope for a viable embryo to transfer three days later. The doctor would make sure my egg and his sperm created the strongest embryo possible.

It sounded simple enough, and we received all the encouragement we needed from the doctor. He kept saying over and over, "You're a perfect candidate!" Built up by his optimism, I couldn't wait for the magic to happen.

In the weeks prior to this, I prepared by doing things that a woman might enjoy if she knew she was going to get pregnant the next month. I took one last dip in the Jacuzzi at our gym. I cut my hair and highlighted it. I drank wine at dinner whenever I felt like it.

With all of these "pre-pregnancy" rituals complete, we began monitoring on day seven of my twenty-eight-day cycle in mid-September. Monitoring entailed visiting the fertility clinic each morning between 7:00 and 9:00 a.m. for a check-in. Kevin came with me every day.

In a waiting room full of baby-making hopefuls, I both hated and loved all of the "success-story babies" that lined bulletin boards in the hallways. Kevin and I would stare off into space or play with our cell phones until my name was called and I went back for blood work and then an internal sonogram. Before long, these procedures were just a part of the process. With the bigger goal in mind, I tolerated bruises on my arm from all the blood draws. Lying on a table with my pants off was my every-morning routine.

Yet, as monitoring days continued, we encountered a bump in the road. Kevin's parents' fiftieth wedding anniversary collided with our IVF calendar. The day before we were to leave for their Georgia town, the fertility clinic called to say I was medically grounded. "You can't fly. We might need to trigger ovulation to collect your egg (*which would include getting a shot in the butt: awesome!*) soon. You're ovulating quicker than we thought!" For one of the first times in my life, it sucked to be an overachiever.

Kevin didn't want to leave me. But how could he *not* go? We'd planned this party for years with his two siblings. It was a party he knew my in-laws had been looking forward to for months. It was a party we needed to attend. But it would be a lot easier to make excuses as to why the daughter-in-law was not there compared to the son. He later told me that he boarded the plane in tears, but he did so with my blessing.

I sent him off because I really I thought I'd be okay at home by myself. I planned to catch up on my favorite household chore—laundry—and enjoy re-runs of TV shows I never had time to watch. Quiet time, I believed, was good for the soul—especially mine. But as I sat on the couch trying to be brave and think of fun things to do, I felt shaky and vulnerable. Our house felt cold without Kevin. I craved the company of not just another person, but a dear friend.

So, with a suitcase packed for a couple of days, I became a fertility refugee out on the open road.

Without any warning, I showed up at Meredith's doorstep. I knew she was in town. We had become those kind of friends that knew each other's schedules well and came over unannounced. However, it was not a convenient weekend for Meredith to host a houseguest, since she had already committed to host a childhood friend from the West Coast in her basement. On top of that, back spasms had flattened her.

But somehow, I had the courage to confess on her doorstep, "I can't go home," and she had the insightful compassion to say, "You can stay here with us. Our couch has your name on it."

As soon as I got my bag inside, Meredith was off to take a nap. I assessed the situation and decided that dinner was in order. Since her cabinets lay bare, I took her fifteen-year-old son Liam with me to the nearby grocery store to shop. I planned a Mexican casserole with salad and a chocolate cake for dessert. Liam's eight-year-old sister, Brianna, helped me with dessert, icing the cake and setting the table. I taught her how to fold the napkins so they lined up with the plates. We unloaded the dishwasher together. An hour later, I woke Meredith to say dinner was ready. We laughed and laughed at the supper table and then decided a movie was in order at a theater within walking distance of their house.

The mood of the evening continued to be light and fun. We all devoured the chocolate cake before bed. I nearly forgot why I was so afraid of the upcoming procedures, breathing in deeply a single word: "Home." Now, all I needed to do was visit the doctor again in the morning for another sonogram and blood sample. Meredith promised to go with me.

The next morning, Kevin called to see how I was doing. He said he could tell by the sound of my voice that I was having fun. It was true: I'd left the doctor's office in a good mood after the weekend doctor said my sonogram looked great. The nurse who checked me out said someone would call in the afternoon with instructions about how to prepare for the egg retrieval on Monday morning. Kevin would be back on Sunday afternoon. Perfect. Game on!

Because the guest preacher had already prepared to serve in my place on Sunday (since I was to be in Georgia at the party), I immersed myself in a book instead of my normal last-minute sermon preparations. I even researched the possibility of going to church on my own the next day. I couldn't remember the last time I had worshiped without being in charge. It could be a fun adventure! Meanwhile, Meredith took Brianna to soccer practice. While she waited on the bleachers we texted about what to cook together for dinner. Steak and mashed potatoes? Or roasted chicken with rice and beans? What a gift to feel welcomed in Meredith's world, as I had been on countless occasions before. Maybe I'd take a nap later? Reading always put me slowly to sleep. But, before I could begin to dream, the phone rang. It startled me awake. "Hello?"

"Ms. Hagan, we're sorry to inform you that your IVF cycle is canceled. Your blood work today shows an LH hormone surge, and we can't retrieve your egg in time to do the planned procedure."

"What? Why??" I exclaimed.

"It's just something that happens from time to time. It's normal 10 percent of the time. You are going to ovulate too soon for us to get the egg out. Sorry you had this bad luck. And sorry it's canceled. You can try again next month, okay? Goodbye."

Click.

Before I had time to think about any sort of appropriate response to the news or consider how the nurse could deliver such a report so insensitively and why in the heck did the doctor not call me himself, my body fell to the ground into a child's pose right there in front of the couch. My feet felt limp. My whimpers turned into full sobbing. All I could think was: "This is it! I am *done* being brave." If all the months of invasive testing and waiting and preparations came to this, I was through! A damn LH hormone surge, which didn't mean something was wrong, but set us back another month?

Liam, a kid normally consumed in his teenaged coolness, found me on the living room floor. He noticed me and sought to console me in the only way that a fifteen-year-old boy can: he stared at me. No words. Yet, he stayed close to protect me. I could see the worry on his face as my tears dripped down my pink sweater, wet stains growing larger by the minute. I knew he was hoping that he didn't have to hug me.

Trying to spare him and myself the awkwardness, I stumbled upstairs to Meredith's room, clutching my cell phone. I crawled from the doorframe to the white fuzzy rug at the foot of her bed. I lay prostrate on the floor, continuing to sob as if sobbing was all I knew how to do.

I called Kevin right away. He didn't answer his phone. After several other calls to family members, I finally reached our brother-in-law and asked him to get word ASAP for Kevin to call me back.

I texted Meredith: "When are you going to be home?"

Waiting on her to write me back, tear drops pooled on the rug and fuzz began to stick to my face. Breathing seemed harder and harder. I began panting like a dog.

Finally, Kevin called back. I uttered words for as long I could form them, all the while remaining face down in the rug. He heard, "Our IVF cycle was canceled," but not much else.

I hung up the phone. I knew his family would love on him. I needed to just be. And, sometime later, as the giant dark cloud hovered over me and the rug, Meredith texted, "I'll be home soon." *What was soon?*

I later learned that several neighbors in the adjoining townhouse had knocked on the door before Meredith came home. They asked Liam if everything was okay. Apparently my cries sounded like someone was dying. And, on the inside, I was.

About thirty minutes later, Meredith burst into her house and ran upstairs to her room, finding me buried in the rug that was now shedding all over me. I could not look at her. Meredith joined me on the floor, bad back or not. Then, before I could say a word, she crawled on top of me and laid her head and upper body on top of my back. She cradled her hands around my face. And she wept too. We both sobbed and sobbed. For a very long time. This loss felt like a failure of epic proportions. An even bleaker darkness rushed in, and I wondered what there was to live for anymore.

Soon white fuzzy parts of the rug covered Meredith's sweat-pants too, matching the state of my tearstained face and hands. I sat up a little. She sat up. She hugged me as I buried my head into her shoulder. I didn't know if I could ever move again as the grief of this loss flowed through me. But no friend or relative had ever hugged me as tight and with such care as she did in these moments. This fact made me want to cry too.

Soon Meredith flew downstairs to secure pajamas from my suitcase by the couch. Arriving with my soft, stretchy pants and a t-shirt in tow, she ordered me to put them on, knowing that without strong words I would have stared at her dumbfounded for hours. Then she whisked me into her bed and tucked me under the covers. Though my crying had subsided a little, I was still struggling to breathe. Meredith's bossiness, which normally solicited *that* face from me, was the only thing capable of moving me from one moment to the next.

Soon she offered me some water and one of her sleeping pills. Sliding to the other side of the bed, she lay down too, holding onto my right arm. There was no mistaking it; I could feel her concern on my elbow. I tried to utter words, to talk about what was going on and what I might do next, but she objected with deeper wisdom, saying: "Now is not the time to talk. Just lie here. I will stay with you until you go to sleep."

Though fidgety and afraid to keep breathing, I was not alone. Meredith's love let me know I was wrapped in the hands of a God who said I was never forgotten. Sleeping drugs and a friend: a divine display of love for me.

As I dozed off, Meredith murmured, "I love you, my friend, and I won't let you go."

I stayed alive and hopeful thanks to her nurture that night.

And though there were many tears and many hours ahead of staring aimlessly out the window, not knowing what this failed IVF meant for our family, not knowing whether we'd try again at all, the grief seemed to be about letting the love in as much as it was about letting the pain out. I didn't need to hide anything from Kevin, as I had already learned, and now there was no hiding my pain from Meredith, either.

While I had never felt so lost, I also knew I'd never felt so found. I could begin to say this is what it feels like to be seen even at my worst. I could begin to say this is what it feels like to be nurtured, as a beloved child of God. I could begin to say this is what it feels like to be accepted at my core. No female friend had ever offered me such a gift. For now, God was not far off. No, thanks to Meredith's care, I could feel God close. For it's true, God is near to the brokenhearted. God did not leave me in my pain alone. And, for the first time in my life, I was on the edge of believing it.

Amazingly, I slept the whole night with Meredith by my side.

Finally Something to Do with All Those Candles

The next morning, I woke up with a dehydration hangover from crying and with a sore neck and shoulders from all that time on the floor. But, by 7:00 a.m., I could not be in bed any longer. I wrapped Meredith's fuzzy brown blanket around me like a cape and plopped myself down in one of the bean bag chairs in the middle of her living room.

Meredith heard me stir and soon followed. She wiped her eyes, blearily asking: "Do you want a cup of coffee?"

"Sure."

Then, I blurted out: "I've been thinking…I know you've wanted me to talk to the doctor about going on depression meds."

Meredith hit the start button on the coffee in the adjoining kitchen and then came to my side of the room, directly facing me from the couch.

I went on: "And I've cut you off."

"Yup. Every time. You like to shut me down."

"Well, maybe now I'm ready. This hurts so much. Do you think a pill might help?" I cried saying these words aloud, taking breaths between each word. Meredith teared up again also. It seemed my sadness reminded her of her great sadness too.

"Depression meds, in my experience, don't make it all better. They're not an end-all fix, but they do take the edge off."

She went on to tell me about how, after a long consultation with her doctor, she'd been on a low dose of anti-depressants since the birth of Brianna. The pill, she said, changed the equation. She'd realized that her natural tendency had always been toward depression and wondered why she'd not asked for help sooner.

"Really?" (I never knew this part of her story.)

"I'm just wired to need a little help, and I think you might be wired like me too."

I squirmed in the beanbag chair, taking a rubber band from my wrist and pulling my curly hair into a ponytail. My eyes found Meredith's and I saw the empathy written all over her face as she pushed her glasses up her nose and pulled her straight brown hair behind her ears.

I made a mental note to call the fertility doctor in the morning. I knew Meredith would be proud of me.

By 12:30 p.m. on Sunday afternoon, I left the warmth of Meredith's house to pick up Kevin from the airport.

So much felt unknown as my head filled with questions: Would he let me see his tears? Would he be mad at me for my great failure? Would he be okay with me falling apart? Most of all, could we carry this pain together? I wasn't sure about anything between us, despite our signatures on the St. Michaels covenant.

Our eyes met outside of the baggage claim door. I turned off our black sedan, even though it was in a no parking zone, and ran toward him. I embraced him like I hadn't seen him in years, holding on tight. Within seconds, though, the police whistle jolted us back into reality. Getting into the car, Kevin asked me what I wanted to do. Neither of us was hungry.

"Maybe we could camp out in the bedroom. It's dark in there. Maybe we could light some candles too. I want to be around candles."

He agreed, though I'm sure he thought I'd lost my mind. Once inside our house, I quickly gathered the tea lights left over from Good Friday services last year and ran upstairs to our bedroom. I scattered them around our dresser tops. I lit ten of them. Kevin followed as a silent observer. Like Kevin, I stripped down to only my underwear and t-shirt, and crawled beside him into our king size bed with fluffy feather pillows all around.

Then the words came. "Why, Kevin, why? Why does baby making have to be so hard?"

"I just don't know, my love. I just don't know." Kevin pulled me close as he spoke.

Within minutes of Kevin wrapping his arms around me, my flood of tears returned. His touch brought it on. Together, we relived the initial shock and pain of this newest loss.

We took turns offering questions to the universe: "Why was the world so mean to us? Why? Why did we have to be among the 10 percent with an LH surge? Why? Why could I not complete even one IVF cycle? This is not fair!"

There were no answers, of course, so I cried until I was all dried up. Kevin just held me.

To pass the time, we stared. The tea lights burned out. Kevin interrupted the silence to offer: "Why don't we try to take a nap, sweetheart? Lie close to me. I'm exhausted. I hardly slept last night. I bet you didn't either…"

I tried for several minutes to sleep. But I couldn't. It was in the darkness of the night that I worked out my problems. Such had been my pattern from a young age. When sleep frustrated me, I'd ask my mom for counsel and she'd say: "If you can't sleep, just lie still. Eventually, your mind will catch up with your body." I recalled this advice again in these moments. But I couldn't lie still, not even next to my Kevin. I could not surrender to this horror that was happening to us! Kevin was out, though, so I slid from the covers and headed downstairs.

The living room seemed cold. Solution: this space needed candles too. Lots of them! Operation candle collection began. Some were scented, others not; some lived in jars, others stood alone on protective plates. I lined them up on our coffee table and lit each one. Soon I had myself an altar. Contentment for the next several hours came through my fixation on each flicker.

Nothing else mattered. The phone rang, but with every ring I hit "ignore." The TV remote lodged between the couch pillows poked into my back, and I let it be. My feet felt cold, even under the blanket on the couch, but it seemed like too much trouble to go and find socks. So there I was.

Kevin trudged down the steps hours later declaring his hunger. He surveyed the pantry and told me we had only iced-over frozen pizzas in the freezer and some almonds and cereal but no milk. So if we wanted more than that we'd have to leave the house to be fed.

I told Kevin I wasn't hungry, but he insisted, "You've got to eat something." He could at least fix the dinner problem.

The next morning, Meredith called. But there was little to say. I called in sick to work and resumed staring at the candles I'd relit. When I wasn't staring at the candles, I fixed my gaze out our living room's large bay window, taking in the autumn foliage falling from our neighbor's large oak trees. By mid-morning, my phone beeped with the notification that I had ten unheard voice messages, but I didn't care. Even if one of those calls told me of a death of a beloved church member, I don't think I would have moved an inch.

But when Lucy called, I answered.

Though we'd hadn't talked in days (unusual for us), I'd also texted her from the fuzz of Meredith's rug to tell her the doctor's news. She was in my small inner circle too. "I'm crying with you, Elizabeth," she wrote back. "This is completely unfair."

Lucy and I met the first day of seminary at Duke. I'd heard about her spunkiness from some mutual friends. "You must look Lucy up," they said, "We think the two of you will hit it off." And we did. We soon started studying together in a small group of other twenty-somethings. I spent more time at her apartment than I did at mine. And by my third year of seminary, Lucy and I lived together and our address was widely known as the place to be on weekends for TV marathons, cookie baking, and basketball game watching. Though our first pastorates out of seminary had taken us to different regions of the country, our strong bond remained. If Lucy called, Kevin usually left the room, saying, "Well, I know you are going to be on the phone for an hour" (or maybe two).

Recently, however, Lucy had begun a new church position as a lead pastor in a community less than an hour away from my house. We both were thrilled to be colleagues who got to see each other on a regular basis. It was usual for Lucy, not yet married, to spend the night in our guest room at least once every other week. Whenever she had meetings in our area, she'd come over the night before. Thankfully, Kevin and Lucy became buds too—always joking around about how much time Kevin took to get dressed in the morning and how he hogged the guest bathroom.

"Hello," I answered.

"What's up?" Lucy wanted to know.

"I'm staring at candles."

"Have you eaten?"

"No."

"Do you have any plans for the afternoon other than staring at candles?"

"No."

"Well, I am going to bring you food."

"Okay." I couldn't tell Lucy no. She wouldn't have tolerated it.

Within an hour, Lucy stood at my door, "Bearing gifts," she said. In one hand, she held a sack with a chicken sandwich and fries from Wendy's and several two-liter bottles of Diet Coke. "Sustenance," she called it. And in the other hand, a queen-size fuzzy blanket from Target.

"You brought me a blanket?"

"I thought having this to wrap up in would help."

"Thank you." I hugged her, "It's just like the blanket I cuddled in at Meredith's house. How did you know?"

"I'm glad you like it," she said simply.

I loved it. Ripping through the cardboard packaging and shredding the black ribbon that held the blanket, folded into a tidy square, I transformed myself into a burrito in seconds. There's a reason that infants like swaddling.

Lucy dropped her purse on the floor. On the couch, she curled up beside me with the blanket. "Why don't you eat your sandwich? It's getting cold." She brought me a plate from the kitchen and placed it in my lap. Depression is as depression does; it consumes you until you can make baby steps toward something else. So I made baby steps toward this chicken sandwich, nibbling a couple of bites. Lucy cheered me on.

Eating something did make me feel as if I had enough strength to talk to her. I narrated the highlights of the weekend so she could make sense of the story in better terms than the few fragmented texts I'd sent. I circled around to the call I needed to make to the fertility doctor about the depression meds. "Would you stay here with me if I call him?" I asked.

"Sure. I'd be glad to. Call now, why don't you?"

I sat cross-legged on the couch with my knees touching Lucy's. I scrolled to the number in my phone and hit "call." The front desk receptionist transferred me. When the doctor said "Hello, Elizabeth," I charged forward immediately. I knew that if I didn't get it all out in one breath, it might not ever come out.

"I don't know if you do this, but I'm calling you to ask for help. I don't know if you prescribe drugs for depression, but I think I need to take something." In between tears, I went on to say, "Bottom line: I am not well. Could you help me?"

And he quickly fired back: "I don't do that kind of thing."

"What?!?"

"Depression meds are overrated. Do you need to talk to someone? We have a social worker that comes to our office once a week. You could talk to her. We send all our patients with mental problems to her."

"No, I have a spiritual director who's also a counselor that I see already. I don't need to see someone else." And it was true; my SD, as I liked to call her, was my lifeline on my worst days, helping me toward a better mental frame of mind.

The doc belly laughed as if I were a young child, "Well, if you don't come to see our mental health professional, then I can't help you."

I hung up on him then and there. If slapping him through the phone had been a possibility, I would have! I ranted to Lucy that he didn't even have the nerve to call me on Saturday to tell me about the failed cycle, as any compassionate doctor would have done, and now he was brushing off my problems with another "one size fits all" solution. I hated him. And hated that my one big dream involved him. I hated that we had chosen him. I did not "have mental health problems." I was going through hell.

Lucy found more tissues around the house somewhere, and passed them to me one by one. "Oh, Elizabeth. What a jerk!"

"Well, what about your family doctor?" Lucy wondered. "Why don't we call her and see when you could get an appointment?"

I thought about it. Maybe. But if I did, this would be my last ask. Lucy found a rubber band in her purse. She got out her brush and pulled my hair, ratted up now from being all day on the couch, into a ponytail on top of my head. She grabbed my hand and squeezed it and said, "You can do this! I'm with you and not going anywhere." So, a lot rode on this one phone call.

My fingers trembled as I hit the buttons of the number on my phone. A sweet grandmotherly voice answered the phone. She told me if I could be there in twenty minutes, the doctor would be glad to see me. I relayed the news to Lucy and right away she jumped off the couch in the direction of my shoes, handing them to me. She offered not only to go with me, but also to drive. "You are such a special driver on good days. I don't want to experience you driving under distress."

We giggled. So true. There was that time I almost killed us at a pastor's conference driving up a mountain...

In the waiting room, Lucy read *Sports Illustrated* while the doctor saw me. I felt safe in her presence right away. "How are things at the church?" she wanted to know. "How is Kevin?" But, before I could answer, the concerned look on her face told me I didn't have to engage in her polite chit chat. She dove into the deeper end of questions about my moods, sleeping and eating patterns. "I'm going to help you," was all I needed to hear. And

I left her office with a prescription for a mild antidepressant and an appointment time for a follow-up consultation.

Lucy celebrated with me in the car. "You did it! I'm so proud of you! Now let's go get the prescription filled!"

Trip to CVS completed, Lucy asked: "What else would make you feel better?"

"Dairy Queen." Two doors down from CVS in the strip mall by our house sat a DQ. And, as a child, a favorite "I'm sick" spot was Dairy Queen. I'd nursed many a sore throat and cold over the years with an Oreo Blizzard. Lucy knew it was my favorite too. She bought me one while I stayed in the car. Who cared that my diet was not balanced? Zoloft went down easier with Oreo cookies mixed in sitting beside this dear one who loved me.

Three months later, Lucy and I chatted on the phone on an average Monday afternoon. The depression meds and I agreed with each other. My mind felt clearer. But, in the time since that day, my body had endured IVF twice more. *Fails, twice more.* The second fail had come because my embryonic cells had ceased to multiply on day two after the transfer, and the third because, two weeks later, I simply wasn't pregnant. However, hope stayed alive in my heart and Kevin's. Our dream of parenthood propelled us forward to whatever the doctor thought we should try next.

As I began to catch Lucy up on the latest, she offered, "Share your narrative." This was a phrase we'd learned in one of our seminary classes that we both thought was hilarious and seemed to stick between us as a joke.

I went straight to it: "Making a baby has broken my heart deeper than I've ever known. But, at the same time, I've also felt more seen and loved by a few of you than I've ever imagined."

I took a breath and then went on, "So I'm thinking that sometimes the only way that real love can go deep down inside of us is for our heart to be cracked open. And through the pain, love has the room to seep into us and live."

The phone line was quite for several minutes and I started to think I was totally off my rocker when Lucy piped in and said,

"That's really beautiful. Really, really beautiful, friend."

"I hate this pain, you know, but I also have never felt so loved. You and Meredith and Kevin are rock stars to me. I don't know what I would think about God these days without you. When I think God doesn't love me I just think of you guys and smile."

Lucy, never one to let the serious mood go on too long, broke out into the Hezekiah Walker gospel classic, "*I need you. You need me. We're all a part of God's body.*" We both giggled as I wiped tears from my face. These were the lyrics of a song we'd been forced to sing to each other at a retreat our first year of seminary. It was "our song" to make each other laugh. But, truth be told, it was how we felt about our friendship.

I wasn't pregnant yet. But a feast of sisters nourished me at every turn. And the tan blanket Lucy brought me never left the couch.

Laughter at the Wailing Wall

When a couple goes through infertility, it's not as if everything else stops. House chores, family, and professional obligations go on. For Kevin and me, remaining present in the "non-fertility-focused" world felt so challenging. We wanted to try, even though we wanted to spend every free moment with the covers over our heads.

When the calendar page turned to 2011, Kevin and I kept our commitment to attend a ten-day interfaith trip to Israel. We were to travel with other local clergy in conjunction with a local university. We'd leave the U.S. the day before Martin Luther King Jr.'s birthday and celebrate the holiday together in Israel, making a statement as Jewish, Muslim, and Christian leaders that people of all faiths could get along in spite of our obvious theological differences. The support and the excitement of the church leadership about this once-in-a-lifetime opportunity spurred me on. Our congregation, the local mosque, and the local synagogue had already made plans to meet together in shared learning upon our return.

When our itinerary arrived in the mail two days after New Year's, I read we'd go to the Western Wall on day two. I was immediately intrigued, remembering its significance from seminary studies. The Western Wall, also known as the Wailing Wall, is the remaining segment of the second Jewish temple, built by Herod the Great. I knew this site drew Jews together from all over the world—to mourn, to pray, and most of all to hope for the future. I excelled at crying, so it sounded like my kind of place!

Around the dinner table later that evening, I shared with Kevin this good news: "Hon, we're going to a wall of tears. Isn't this great?" He nodded in affirmation, his way of saying back to me, "I'm glad you are excited about something."

I'd read that a meaningful part of the experience for many included placing prayers in the cracks of the wall. In the weeks before we left—in response to our invitation—countless friends and church members had given us prayers rolled up in small pieces of paper to take with us to the Wall. Why not make this stop on our trip a communal exercise? Though I hadn't opened any out of respect for confidentiality, I knew some of the prayers were about unruly teenage children from frazzled single mothers. I knew some requests hoped for healing from cancer. I knew some prayers were pleas for unemployed family members to find jobs. You don't go to the Wall with just any prayer, it seemed. Tremendous burdens resided in these fragments of paper.

But, what about me? Would I take a prayer? In my moments of quiet reflection as I thought about all the sorrow of the past year, as well as the latest string of friends who had made social media declarations of motherhood, I knew I needed to write my own prayer. No ordinary prayer would do. I began drafting with my mind made up. I'd go to Israel prepared.

Upon arrival, in preparation for our first full day of traveling in Jerusalem's old city, our tour guide, Aziz, took me aside. He explained that as the only female in the group, I'd be alone during our prayers at the Wall. "Men are on one side and women are on the other. It's the Orthodox way."

I assumed I would meet the segregation of the Wailing Wall with frustration, hurt, and annoyance. "Why can't I go pray with the men, especially with my husband?" I wanted to scream. I am a feminist, after all. I believe my self-worth is no less than any man's.

However, as I walked into the temple court and around the metal dividers that directed me to the women's side, I found tears welling up in my eyes for a completely different reason.

Right away, I felt at home. I was glad to be surrounded only by fellow females, my sisters in humanity.

Taking a few deep breaths, aware of each step bringing me closer to the Wall, there was something incredibly holy that came over me as I surrendered to whatever the experience could offer. Though seemingly just a bunch of old rocks, I knew these were the stones that told the story of the faith tradition that gave my spirit life. I knew that thousands upon thousands of pilgrims like me had entered this Plaza with heavy hopes on their shoulders—in sadness for what might have been, bearing prayers for the nation of Israel, or carrying great requests: problems too big for human hands to hold any longer.

The space felt incredibly safe and inviting, even though I was a Christian pastor dressed in jeans and a beige sweater under a heavy black and white checkered overcoat, no prayer book in my grasp. No chants in Hebrew (Baptists could opt out of this class at my seminary) would come from my mouth. Instead, I attended to the task at hand. I pulled the rustling strips of prayers out of my coat's front pocket. And then I found mine buried under my water bottle at the bottom of my oversized pink purse. Folding it over several times, as if I was making origami, I wedged it into the wall the best I could without ripping the sheet of paper. My soul lay open between the rocks:

I am a Mother.

Yet in my house there are no stray toys rolling around on the floor. There are no sippy cups with apple juice residue piled up by the sink. There are no schedules of what child goes where and when on our refrigerator. There are no school papers stacked on our kitchen table or science project parts strewn across our countertops.

I am not identified in any communities of mothers. I am not invited to forums of mothers who work outside the home. I've never read What to Expect When You Are Expecting, *or gone to a play group with girlfriends and their kids. I cringe when I am asked by strangers: "How many kids do you have?" Why? Because I always have to say, "I have none."*

Rather, my home life is as adult-centered as it comes. Almost never do you find my husband and me sitting at the kitchen table at mealtimes. You wouldn't find child-protective devices on our electrical outlets or wine cabinet doors, nor do we sketch out our weekend activities around nap times or soccer games. And there are empty rooms in our home, two of them. Though we've planned big, it is still just the two of us.

But, I am a Mother. I have children...

...But no one sees them. There are those who have dwelled within me, but decided to take a short, in fact very short, stay. And I wouldn't have known about them either, except for the signs that pointed to their dwelling. My body spoke of them through exhaustion, nausea, and cravings of unusual foods. Something new had found its way into me, and my heart counted the days and yearned for them to stay, even—just even—for one more day. I loved them, each one of them.

And when they were gone, making their way out of me like a disgruntled houseguest, I wept. I cried tears so big they ran from my cheeks to my navel. They poured like an upstream river out of my being. I didn't know when or if the intense pain would ever stop. I couldn't believe that such a good gift could be so cruelly taken so soon. Yet, these children were never gone from my heart. I was still their Mother.

Yet, there remain in this time and space children of mine who I do not mother alone. Some have blonde hair, some have dark skin; some are very young, and others are much older than me in years but alone in their own way. Each is searching for spaces in this crazy world to call their own and for someone to recognize who they really are. They cry out and, even though my own pain sings a loud song, I do hear them. It is my honor to see them. I fiercely want to protect them from any more of life's deepest pains. I love them and weep for them too—not because their life has gone from me, rather because it has come and stayed close. They have come into my heart and they are now part of me too. Our bond is undeniably good.

So, no, I may never be able to attend the innocence of the average baby shower with other mothers-to-be, or be invited to a mother's support group, or even be able to talk fully about my mothering pain and joy in public. I am learning to accept that the gift of mothering I have been given may never be understood by most. And I might never know what physical life coming from my womb is like. Such is the cost of unconventional motherhood: loneliness.

Yet, no matter how I feel or what others say or even what the future may hold for me, there is one thing I know: I am, and will always be, a mother.

As I emptied my soul of these words, a great sense of relief came over me. Though my instinct was to take the prayer out of the wall and cherish my words again, I just couldn't. The prayer sat in the cracks of the Wall. It was no longer my burden to carry. My worries belonged to God.

Soon after this prayer surrendering process, I felt a strong need to cover my head with the floral red scarf I'd brought along while I sat in one of the white plastic chairs close to the wall. There was no official who asked me to cover my head, as had been the case with the site we visited the day before, but it seemed like the right thing to do. To cover my head allowed me to take in what being at a site full of so many hopes, so many sorrows, and so many worries meant for generations before me right then at that very moment.

As I looked with tears rolling down my cheeks at the crowd of my sisters that surrounded me, I was truly glad that no men were present. Maybe someone was crying tears from a font similar to mine? Who knows? There are unique sorrows in what it means to be a woman, and it felt right to be able to grieve alongside those who could understand me the most.

I saw an African woman kneeling, leaning toward the wall, praying with a rosary. I saw a Euro-American woman kissing the wall as if it were her long-lost lover. I observed a woman with Down syndrome embracing a teenage traveling companion, so overcome by sadness that she could hardly stand, weeping into her arms. I saw a Jewish woman, prayer book in hand, rocking back and forth with more devotion toward a holy book than I've ever seen by my peers toward any Christian text.

And I didn't want to leave. I wanted to stay and cry and cry and truly invite any sadness in me to come out and be gone. I was tired of it. Yet the longer I sat in the chair, the more I felt the Spirit saying to me, "Get up. Go in peace. You've grieved enough."

I walked out into the courtyard to find Kevin and the others. Right away, Kevin noticed: "There's something different about you. Are you okay?"

I was more than okay. Spontaneously, I started humming the song "Peace like a River," for which I'd learned motions as a child. In an instant, where tears had flowed minutes earlier, calm warmed my weary bones. Soon my steps felt lighter. Back in the van, I talked with my colleagues, fully engaged in the expectation of the journey ahead. The words "peace sacrament" rose to my lips. I knew God have given me peace at that wall as a sacrament, a means of grace. But, what's that? Baptists as a whole, after all, don't even claim the word *sacrament*. We talk instead about ordinances, and there are only two of them: baptism and the Lord's supper. So, then, how in the world could I begin to talk about the Holy I had encountered at the Wall? It didn't really matter, I realized; it just *was*.

As the trip continued, we ate our way through the nation. I learned that in Israel hospitality exists as a supreme virtue, much like the rest of the Middle East. In particular, dinners in Israel (and most lunches, for that matter) were long affairs. Abundant bread, hummus, and cheese filled the long tables. We'd clean our plates only to find them filled up again. As we ate together as a group, conversation with one another became our entertainment. Aziz and our other guide, Elad, told us tales of their adventures as peacemakers during times of war, while the rest of us sipped on wine. We breathed in the slower pace of life in this country.

Any time the American rabbi in our delegation chimed in on the conversation with an anecdote of some kind, I couldn't help but giggle. His sarcastic humor was just my style. And, even before the story's punch line, I belly laughed in response. My laughter became contagious. Night after night I erupted in laughter and the rest of the restaurant followed. The group started to anticipate it and look forward to its arrival. I became known as "The Laughing Reverend." I was unstoppable! From sullen girl on the couch to the life of the party in Israel—things just kept getting stranger and stranger.

I recognized for the first time, after all of those sermons I'd heard on her, why Sarah laughed when God told her she'd have a baby. Laughter can be a response to surprise or disbelief, yes, but it can also just be comfort in your own skin.

Most of all, I knew this: the spiritual rocks in my soul had moved. The wind of the Spirit was blowing within me, and, for the first time in months, my feet stood on fertile ground. I was coming home to earth again, for even though nothing about our dreadful situation had seemed to change, at least according to our medical files, something had changed in me.

Why Don't You Just Adopt?

After we returned from Israel, we began sharing our baby-making woes with a few more people. I can't tell you how many well-meaning people stopped me mid-story and asked, "Why don't you just adopt?... Really, Elizabeth, why don't you just find yourself a baby to adopt? Babies who need homes are everywhere, aren't they?"

My heart sank a little more each time I heard the question and the commentary to follow. These questions felt like someone trying to offer me a sorry-you-don't-get-to-have-a-baby "Let's Make a Deal" consolation prize. And I hated it. I hated it every time. Not because I was anti-adoption, but because the question felt like a Band-Aid, an attempt to cover pain I never asked for or wanted. Did friends not know how much vulnerability it took to share even a fraction of my story? I just wanted to be heard, and then for the conversation's subject to be changed back to a more communal topic.

But it was true: Kevin and I came into marriage saying we'd adopt one day. We both loved the idea of helping a child or children who needed a safe home and a loving place to grow up. We knew we could be *that* kind of parents—parents who loved any child, even if the child was not biologically ours. I'd traveled extensively internationally, meeting children in the worst possible living conditions, many without parents to look after them. I hoped I could make a difference in just one life through adoption. However, at *that* point our plan had been to consider this *after* having children of our own. Neither of us were getting any younger. We needed to attend to what our bodies could produce first.

But, after all the failure we'd experienced in "fertility land," I began thinking, "Well, maybe... We *could* alter the plan. Isn't that what always happens? You adopt a baby and then you surprisingly get pregnant?"

We had a great contact for an adoption attorney, so this eased our minds. We could talk to her. What would a meeting hurt? And it wouldn't be like trying too hard. I called and scheduled our "get to know you free of charge" meeting. *How exciting that something was free!*

On a sunny spring morning, Kevin and I pulled up to the home office of Carol, the partner of one of Kevin's coworkers, and a family friend. Carol was tall and blonde with blue eyes and a bright smile. Though we'd experienced her over the phone as direct and no-nonsense—just as you'd expect most lawyers to be—we also felt from the moment we walked in that she cared about us. "Could I get you something to drink? Could I help you with your coats? Could I offer you a cookie? I just baked some."

And, as we drank our hot tea and munched on chocolate chip cookies on the plates before us, I silently prayed. If we were doing this, then, "Lord Jesus, let this be easy. Let this feel right from moment one. Give Carol the Magic 8 ball with just the right answer for us!"

Our consultation began with Carol soliciting personal information: full names, birthdays, occupations, and contact information, writing it all down on a yellow legal pad. Then, like a sharp turn around a mountain, her questions became more personal. "Could you tell me about your fertility history?"

I thought. *Oh, man. Well, here we go!*

And like water gushing from a newly formed mountain stream, the struggle, the heartbreak, and all the accompanying details we'd shared with only a few flowed out of Kevin and me. We took turns relaying details. This spacious living room became a place we could explode safely. Carol got it all, bless her. (Thank goodness we weren't paying her by the hour *yet*.)

"Well, wow, what a journey you've been through already!"

To ease our sharing, she confided in us about her own difficulties in conceiving. She'd undergone IVF three times before getting pregnant with her now seven-year-old son. When Carol said, "I know how you feel," I trusted her. All three of us shared membership in the same sorority.

Carol started the basic spiel about options for adoption (domestic and international, agency and private, and open and closed) as she handed us a box of Kleenex from across the table. Conversations of this magnitude did not come without tears. In clearly drawn charts and graphs, she shared how we'd proceed with any option. With our heads overflowing with new information, we had much to ponder as we drove into work late that morning. So much.

As for me, it felt like perfect timing that I'd already made plans to hang out with Meredith after work. I'd warned her about the adoption attorney meet-up. I knew she'd want to know more about the big talk and how I felt about it.

As I walked in Meredith's door, before I had time to take off my shoes, she gestured, "Help, help," motioning me into the kitchen. I jogged in her direction. She gave me a spoon and said, "Stir," while she buttered the rolls.

Standing over the cheese sauce as it slowly simmered on the stove, I told her something in my gut was telling me that an adoption opportunity was on its way to us soon. Nothing about our meeting with Carol scared us. I felt like we could totally adopt! Even in those moments of saying my thoughts aloud for the first time, I realized how excited I already felt. I really could see myself as an adoptive mother *now*, not later.

Meredith told me that no matter what Kevin and I decided, she was totally on our team.

Several nights later, Kevin came home with some news from work. One of his closest colleagues, who knew about our struggles, had taken Kevin aside in the break room. His colleague started right in with it: "I know that this is a sensitive issue. And I wouldn't have even approached you if I didn't feel strongly about it, but I just have had you and Elizabeth on my mind, and I need to tell you something as a friend."

"Okay, what is it?" Kevin asked her.

"Well, the son of one of our best friends recently told his dad that he's gotten a girl pregnant. He's nineteen, a college-drop out, and his girlfriend, twenty-three, works at Chili's. She's already had two kids that she gave up. They want to have an abortion."

"And…"

"I know I shouldn't have said anything, but I told the boy about you and Elizabeth. I told him that you and Elizabeth would be great parents. The best, really. And that he and his girlfriend have options if they want to keep the baby. I told the boy not to make a stupid, rash decision."

I knew where this conversation was heading, and my mind went there immediately.

What if? Could I be this baby's mother? Was this just what God had for us—to adopt *this* baby, just like I thought might happen a few days ago? The timing gave me chills.

I'd always said during my more mystical moments in this process, "If we found a baby dropped at our doorstep, I'd be thrilled!" I knew there was no part of Kevin and me not open to children from wherever. No matter how they found their way to us, we absolutely knew we'd welcome them.

And just like my fantasy, here we were with a potential adoption situation dropped on Kevin's work doorstep. So of course we'd say yes! And how perfect that we'd already met an adoption attorney. I always liked being five steps ahead. Kevin's smile told me he was excited even before the word *adoption* came from either of our lips.

As I cleared the supper table and washed the dishes later, as much as I felt hope, I also felt doubt and worry. We'd already received a briefing from the attorney about warning signs. What if this baby was born addicted to meth? What if this kid had special needs as a result of lack of prenatal care? What if this young mother or father didn't like us—how would we feel then? What if the grandmother stepped into the middle of the legal process to say she wanted to raise the baby? They were all valid concerns. Our minds kept racing well into the night.

Over the next couple of weeks, Kevin continued talking to his coworker about this "situation," hoping to learn more details and that no one overheard. We both prayed that this young father and mother would not choose abortion. And most of all we prayed that they'd pick us as the mom and dad.

Then, three weeks after we first learned of this family, something concrete finally happened. Kevin learned the young father wanted to meet us. We sounded like an interesting couple. There had not been an abortion.

Politically, I'd proclaimed myself in the pro-choice camp for years. I believed (and still do) that every woman would be responsible for her own choices before God one day. But as for me, I didn't envision a situation where I would ever abort a healthy baby. Kevin and I wanted so badly to be parents. Other couples like us would like to be parents too. This baby in utero would have a good home with us. So this was a celebratory moment indeed!

I texted Lucy immediately: "No abortion!!" She knew what this meant. Not only was a life saved, but *we* might be getting a baby!

I called Carol right away too. I wanted to know next steps and the protocol for such an encounter. I knew nothing. Carol advised that Kevin go solo and have a talk with the father alone. Since our mutual friend knew this dad-to-be, it seemed best, she said, that Kevin be the one to make the first move, not both of us.

Kevin felt hesitant about getting involved so early, and I was sad I couldn't go with him, but we trusted Carol's judgment. The mother was only three months along in her pregnancy, but it was time to state our serious interest. This couldn't happen if one of us didn't show up.

A week later, the day of the man-to-man coffee meeting came. Kevin left for Starbucks a couple miles away. I curled up on the couch. My channel surfing landed me on *The Bachelor* and its very long rose ceremony. I stared mindlessly at the TV screen. All I could think about was that I wasn't at Starbucks with Kevin. I also knew my husband's larger-than-life personality could impress with flying colors. I voiced silent prayers for discernment and for my heart not to be broken *again*. But most of all, I prayed for Kevin to be fabulously charming.

I finished the episode and then called Lucy to pass the time, bringing her up to date on the latest. She fired back: "Are you sure you're ready for all of this? I mean, I know other couples that have been through this, and it's exhausting."

"Of course I am. Have you ever seen me back away from a challenge?"

Lucy heard me, but I wasn't so sure she was convinced. After all, she'd been the shoulder I'd cried on a so many times in the past couple of months. I think she feared that if this didn't work out, I'd crumble even more.

After two long hours, the phone rang. Without taking a breath, Kevin told me about how he and this young kid had talked about everything under the sun. From music to sports to even hopes and dreams for the future—they covered it all. In summary, it sounded a lot like a big brother sort of conversation, more than it did a "we want to adopt your future child" kind of talk. This worried me. Why did Kevin not press him more? Where was the boy's head in all of this? I wanted to know.

"It just wasn't the right time, Elizabeth," Kevin fired back. "I wanted him to trust me first. He just wanted to get to know me. I could tell he wanted his child to go to someone who shared similar hobbies."

"You don't have any hobbies!"

"Oh, that's not true… I keep us up to date on music, don't I?"

"I'll give you that, but you aren't into sports or outdoor things. So did you fake it well?"

Kevin chuckled. "Yeah, baby, I tried. For us, I tried… You know I used to go hiking in college, so I brought up that."

"I'm sure you did. Making the most of that *one* time you went hiking." I didn't know whether to laugh or cry.

Kevin relayed that he thought the boy liked him, was going to tell his girlfriend about the conversation they shared, and that he'd be in touch. We both agreed there was nothing more we could do. We'd just have to wait it out and see what came next.

I hung up with Kevin and called Meredith right away. "You're never going to believe this, but I think Kevin just met our baby daddy, and they bonded!" I filled Meredith in on the details and asked her to pray.

"You know it's hard for me to be hopeful about anything anymore. But I'm trying. I feel my heart leaping in this direction. Will you pray?"

"Of course I will, but I'm worried, Elizabeth."

"About what? This all sounds good to you, doesn't it?"

"Yeah, it's promising, but still I'm concerned. It might work out. It might not."

Little did she know that this was the second time I'd heard this sort of declaration in the past two hours! My head dropped more into the couch. If my best friends didn't believe, how could I? And by the time Kevin's car pulled up in the driveway I felt like a wet noodle. And of course wet noodles go straight for the nearest bag of potato chips.

But by the next day, my courage had returned. We learned through a phone call to Kevin from the boy that the boy and the girlfriend were really, really interested. Our hearts swelled with joy. We knew the risks of adoption, of course, but we also knew the possibilities. Our bad luck had to turn around at some point. In my head I was already picking girl names. My intuition said this kid would be a girl. Our girl. Madelyn. I'd always wanted a little girl named Madelyn.

We met with Carol again to walk through the process, learning more about laws in the state of Virginia. She gave us names of home study agencies that would help us complete the necessary paperwork to be cleared for an adoption process to move forward when the time came. I sent off for paperwork from all three groups on her list and eagerly waited for the mail. Our new family motto: *All energy toward adoption*. Never was I so excited about paperwork in my life!

The thick packets of paperwork came in the mail and I started filling them out right away, ignoring the bulletin due to the church secretary in a couple of hours. Game on. I put in a frozen pizza for dinner and I'd just brought up a load of clean clothes to fold from downstairs when Kevin's phone rang. He didn't answer the call because he was in our bedroom upstairs putting on his pajamas for the night. He came down the stairs and played the voicemail. It was from baby daddy.

Kevin put it on speakerphone, and all I heard was: "I've decided to raise my child."

Our adoption dreams died with these words.

Though he and his girlfriend had already broken up and he had little money to pay for much of anything, he wanted to keep his kid. And of course, this was their choice to make.

The mercy of the process was that by this time we were only four-and-a-half months in, but the sting of what would not be burned deep. So much for adoption being anything near easy!

Through my tears, I reminded myself that this was why I had gone through the pain of all of the IVF shots and pills. If one day a procedure actually worked, then one day a kid would come out of *my body* and nobody would question whether or not he or she *was mine*. And nobody would try to take it away from us! I would be the child's momma. And Kevin would be the child's daddy. And that's all I really wanted.

8

Escaping to the Desert

After such a heartbreaking loss on top of a year of fertility doctor visits and two years in total "trying" to get pregnant, my grief of needed to go somewhere. And, as we looked to the possibility of fertility treatment #4 with my biological clock ticking away, my grief kept bubbling over. The mantras I'd employed in the past to keep me focused weren't working. Words I'd said over and over while driving to work or brushing my teeth, such as, "You're strong. Just push on through," or, "You can do this alone," or, "Who cares how much pain you're in? Care for others!" amounted to rubbish. I just could not fake it anymore. I needed something to look forward to other than the next High Holy Day at the church. I needed to feel something in my body again.

My quest for a distraction began with: "If you could go anywhere or do anything, what would you do?" And all my answers came back to the spa. I loved the spa. It was a complete treat I saved for my birthday or Christmas gift each year. And as our infertility season plodded on, a well-kept spa was the one place I felt connected to my body anymore.

Among infertility's many insults was how it wanted to take away my body. At the doctor's office, my body became an object to be poked, prodded, and manipulated. At home, my body belonged to well-timed sex whether I was in the mood or not. Then, at some point during the month, my body bore the shame of a period. In all of these things, I hated my body. I hated my body for not giving me what so many women my age seemed able to do without even trying. I hated my body for its label of "less than."

But the spa was different. No one ever took blood from my arm there. No one asked me to take off my clothes to examine my body. No one extracted my eggs as I lay still. The spa welcomed my body back to the land of normal. There, people wanted me to feel comfort. They wanted me to be relaxed. They wanted me to tell them exactly how I felt, whether the pressure of the massage was too hard or too soft. In those sacred moments of no longer bearing the humiliating pain of "infertility land," God came near.

On one such outing during the week of my thirty-first birthday, I met God in a quiet room. Sitting alone, I waited for my name to be called for a massage, and I began to meditate. I let the quiet of the space wash over me. And out of the silence came a word that I could hardly believe: "One day you'll have a child." Over and over again, these words rose to the front of my conscious. This time, they felt different. Sure, my close friends always said, "I know you'll be a mom. I believe." But hearing them now, I received them differently. Though the rational part of me wanted to call this crazy, some deep intuition said: "Stop, Elizabeth, and listen."

And I did.

So, in my search for a distraction, joy, and maybe even more words from God in this ongoing drama, perhaps I needed to go to the spa again.

Meredith and her adventure-loving self came to mind right away as a perfect companion. She loved the spa as much as I did, if not more. Long day trips to get massages in our city became a regular part of the glue that held our friendship together. If we hadn't seen each other or spent quality time in conversation in a while, one of us would find a way to propose a visit even if it was just for a $20 manicure.

While daydreaming about possibilities, brilliance came. Hours later, when Kevin walked in the door after work, I burst out with excitement: "Sedona, Arizona! I need to plan a trip to Sedona! Meredith and I need to go to Mii Amo spa for a week. This is what I want to do. It would make me really happy!"

I knew of Mii Amo because Kevin and I had spent a couple of days there two years earlier. Set at a high elevation 115 miles north of Phoenix, Sedona is a medium-sized, retirement-friendly town with a claim to fame as one of the center points of the earth's "energy fields." Sedona is a place to which tourists and faith seekers with open minds come to re-group, re-center, and find inspiration as they stroll one of the town's acclaimed "vortex walks," places where the energy points of the earth are said to converge. The red clay, the million-year-old rock formations, the dry heat, the friendliness of the locals—all these things welcome tourists with wonder. New Agers love Sedona, so it might not be the place you'd expect a Christian pastor to admire. But, after visiting once, I no longer called it a New Age town. I called it paradise. I started saving for a return trip as soon as I got home, tucking honorariums received for officiating weddings into an envelope in my sock drawer labeled "Sedona Fund." In the ongoing fertility drama, however, I had forgotten all about my secret stash. What joy I felt to remember!

Returning home from dinner that night, I ran upstairs to our bedroom to find it. I counted the tens, twenties, and hundred dollar bills I'd stashed away. When added up, it was more money than I'd expected! Though I wanted to object to my own plan, saying now was not the time to spend money on something for myself, I just couldn't let this idea go away. I priced hotel reservations and Kevin volunteered some of his airline miles for the cause. When I checked in with Meredith, her enthusiastic "When can we leave?" brought joy to my face. I felt so honored that Meredith said yes. A week to be with me, just me, leaving her family at home. I couldn't believe it! And the dream came together. I wrote "Sedona or Bust" on the April calendar.

Meredith and I made our way to Sedona after a stopover in Phoenix. Within a couple of hours, we settled into the Sedona vibe, opening ourselves to whatever this adventure entailed. First rule: no counting calories. After checking into our hotel, we hit a grocery store to buy potato chips, Diet Coke, and cookies for the room. Meredith said, "You must buy at least one of your favorite junk foods." I picked out strawberry Pop Tarts. I felt like a five-year-old…a happy one!

Over the next four days at Mii Amo, we ate breakfast at a leisurely pace. We found the best spots around the pool and read *People* magazine till we were caught up on "who wore it best" in the last six months. We sat in the hot tub till our toes looked like prunes, and stared a lot at the breath-taking views of the canyons from our room's patio. On day one we thought we'd take a hike to work off some of the calories, but only made it through the children's trail (sort of). We retreated back to "our spot" and sat by the pool again for hours. We let ourselves be engulfed in hues of orange, red, and grey. On this unbelievable gift of a trip, my sadness felt as far away as I was from home and next Sunday's sermon.

Meredith and I were sometimes quiet, but mostly not. We talked deeply about what the real stuff of life is made of: marriage, family, work, her children, and hypotheses about the future paths of our individual lives and careers. The more we talked, the safer I felt. Meredith cradled my words with compassionate listening as I sought to do the same for her.

Over breakfast on the second day, Meredith, the brave one, asked: "How about we pick out a spa experience to do together? What about something that is totally 'Sedona' that we'd never go for any other time?"

I agreed to at least look at the "Other Experiences" page in the resort booklet, envisioning options such as "hula healing" or bird calling or other things that would be totally out of my physical or spiritual comfort level. There would no way I'd say yes to something like that. But then Meredith read from the Reiki section. The booklet said: "Reiki focuses on centering energy through healing palms."

"Can you do this, E?" We laughed. I said no.

Meredith fought back, "Oh, come on, E!"

"Well, okay—if nothing else, at least I'll get a good blog out of this."

Within the hour, we were leaning on the marble counter at the front desk and scheduling our joint appointment for the next morning.

The next day dawned, and at several minutes before 11:00 a.m. we changed into the required robes, giggling about what our Reiki experience would entail.

Punching in the code to her locker, Meredith said bossily, "You aren't allowed to look at me when she brings out the healing palms, okay?"

I agreed. The two of us could get into a lot of trouble if we started laughing. But upon first sight of the therapist assigned to our joint experience, I knew this wasn't a joke. She was a grey-haired woman in her sixties with a name tag that said ten years of service on it. She walked with a stand-up straight sort of posture as she quickly guided us both to an outside cabana facing the Red Rock Canyon. With the clock approaching midday, the sun shone directly overhead. Ravens flew in between the rocks. Lizards ran from the ground, scurrying as far up the canyon as our eyes could follow. The canyon's glare blinded us if we stared at it too long. Soon, we were told exactly what to do:

"Take a seat, Meredith and Elizabeth, on those two stools facing the canyon."

"I will not laugh. I will really not laugh," I kept saying under my breath in Meredith's direction.

After some brief introductions about our hometown and occupations and some moments of silence, the therapist asked each of us to stand. I shifted away from my childish impulses and toward intentional listening. I would give this experience a chance.

The session started with our eyes closed. The grey-haired lady spoke: "I want you to imagine a beam of golden light on the top of each of your heads. As you imagine this light, I want you to visualize where it goes in you—how far the light flows down into your body as I place my healing hands close." I expected that the therapist would somehow touch me. Isn't this what massages are about? But that is not the Reiki way. Turns out, much of it is a hands-free exercise based on the intuitive gifts of the therapist.

After several minutes imagining this hypothetical light over me, I realized it only went as far as the top of my head. I shared my response, and then the therapist shared hers. "I only see the light going as far as your throat." Though I had no idea whether questions were allowed, I quickly fired back even with closed eyes: "What do you mean, my throat?"

"The light around you, above you, has not made it yet to your voice. You are holding back expression of yourself."

Immediately, this all got real. I began to weep. This woman I'd met only ten minutes earlier had touched something in me deeper than words, something I didn't even know was true until the moment she uttered it. She was right: I didn't trust my own voice. I was afraid to speak what I really wanted. I was afraid that my most true words would hurt others. The light stopped glowing beyond my head.

After Meredith's turn to imagine and share where the light seeped into her, tears continued to stream down my face and, I knew, down hers too. (*She was never a quiet crier, either.*) Then the therapist began to ask each of us a series of deeper questions that we weren't meant to respond to aloud.

"What holds you back? Why can't the light get into you? What if you began to live with the light in the very place that it stopped in you?"

With really wet cheeks by this point, God and I had a moment. With Meredith's gift of secure presence by my side, courage came to go *there*—to a very deep place of self-reflective honesty. This is what I knew: I wasn't just a little afraid; I was deathly afraid. I was afraid to love. I was afraid that who I was made to be was not acceptable. I was afraid to use my voice to say what I wanted to say.

After years and years and years of trying to connect with others in such failed ways, I had long ago stopped using the voice in me that spoke the truth. Truth like, "Could we be real friends?" Truth like: "I want to be held." Truth like: "What I need in my life is more than a baby to call my own." Most of all, I never knew how to speak the uninhibited words of "I love you" whenever I felt like saying it.

Instead, my life game plan consisted of becoming the best imitation of me that could be deemed socially acceptable. I did not send emails I wanted to send. I did not kiss dear ones goodbye on the check. I did not call people when I thought of them. I feared my love was too much. I feared I wasn't good enough at being me.

But, what if? What if, like the therapist said, I held back no more?

I was dying inside and had been for a long time. But, instead of continuing to carry the grief, hope came over me. I stared ahead to the canyons, keeping close to the therapist's truth-telling words. I knew I was in love. I was in love with the idea of life without the gates I'd built around my heart to keep me safe. I was in love with how much joy might be rising up to meet me. I was in love with a future I couldn't control, even with dreams of motherhood set aside for a moment.

In this love, I wanted to be a woman who didn't fear telling people how much she loved them. I wanted to be a woman who didn't fear getting close to those who seemed to love her most. I wanted to be a woman who could confidently claim that her voice was powerful, even in the midst of trouble in baby-making land that rendered her powerless in that aspect of her life.

In all these things, visions of joy I did not yet know sprung from me. Maybe, just maybe, the world was missing out on some of the greatest contributions I could offer? Maybe there was light in my voice? Maybe others needed to hear what I had to say as much as I needed to speak it? Just letting my mind go to these thoughts lightened the load.

When it was time to leave the cabana, not only did my tears vanish but my soul smiled. I believe the therapist saw it too, in my eyes. On the way out, she hugged me tight and gave me a look that said, "I'm so grateful I could help." I hoped my smile said thank you enough.

Breaking our silence of the holy over loaded nachos back by the pool, I blurted out, "There are no words. Wow."

Meredith smirked: "She so liked you better than me. Not fair."

Changing gears, Meredith looked me straight in the eyes and moved her body toward me in a serious listening posture: "Tell me about it. What happened to you today? Seemed sort of serious."

I didn't want Meredith to think I was crazy. We'd planned to make fun of this experience, after all, not be changed by it. But something prodded me to go for it. In that moment, I knew what I had to say even as terror lodged on my lips: "I am so afraid that my love is going to hurt people."

Meredith got it right away. She knew that I was expressive, communicative, and sensitive to feelings. She knew I had grown up in a community where I never quite fit in, with years of loneliness a huge part of my story. She knew my mind filled with soulful words that I needed to speak in the direction of others that could be really helpful. Bottom line, she knew me.

I continued on: "I'm afraid if people like you and Kevin and Lucy knew how much I loved you, you'd leave me."

"Are you kidding me?" she asked. "I've been crying all morning thinking I'm a bad mom, and you're afraid that you love people too much?"

"Well, yeah." We laughed. Then, I went back to crying. "My love hurts people because I just love so much."

Looking me straight in the eyes, Meredith soon added: "You can love me all you want, dear friend. Don't you know how much I need *you* in my life too? You've got some pretty awesome and intense people in your life now, people who are like you. Trust us. We're not going anywhere."

Feeling as though my heart might burst if we kept up this kind of sharing for much longer, I directed the conversation elsewhere. "Our morning with the Reiki lady gave me something to think about."

"What?" Meredith wanted to know.

"I'm going to write a book about our fertility story."

A radiant beam exploded across her face. "I've known all along you'd need to write about this," she responded. "I'm so glad. It'll be a very important story to tell."

I traveled home with courage and hopes for a new kind of life. I wanted others to love me deeply. I wanted to love others deeply in return. Yes, I still wanted a baby, but I had just signed up for a far bigger birth.

9

The Day Someone Offered Me Their Sperm

Sedona led me to a fertile land called "Get Real." My new mantras: "Speak up. Show up. Love greatly." As exciting as this all was, threads of my own grief kept pulling me down. The hardest part: I couldn't find communities of friends with whom to be real! Everything about the friendship circles I'd previously loved kept changing. My friends kept having babies. I didn't want any more of my friends to have them till I did. Case closed! (*If life were only this easy!*)

But because I wanted to be brave, I tried. Overcoming my pain was so much harder than I ever imagined. I'd vow to take a pregnant friend out to lunch, but the morning of, I'd make up an excuse to cancel. I'd show up for dinner club with our "with children" friends, but I'd run to the bathroom in between courses dissolving into a puddle of tears, begging Kevin to leave ASAP. I'd RSVP "Yes" for a baby shower but end up putting my present in the mail a week later. Their joy, their round bellies, their infants feeding at their breasts—all this escalated my pain. I could not find any way around it. I did not want to see pregnant women or young mothers unless they were members of my church. I knew this resolve might continue to assassinate my social life at the ripe old age of thirty-two, but I accepted it. The alternative felt worse. A world filled with baby bottles, strollers, and tiny booties felt like a bad dream that I could not shake.

But, then, Marie told me she was pregnant. Five months pregnant. Five months pregnant after trying to be pregnant for four years. Two years longer than I'd waited. I could not blow her off in the same way. We'd been friends for at least fifteen years, making her my oldest friend. My run-and-hide routine would not work so well on her.

Marie and I first met during our freshman year while hanging out in a mutual friend's college dorm room. Marie, a medium-height, strawberry blonde, never-met-a-stranger-type, fire-powered leader, often reminds me now that I wasn't too friendly on this first encounter. "You didn't say more than a couple words to me the first time we met," Marie says. True enough. I admired her too much to know what to say. At eighteen, Marie's perfectly balanced schedule plus her confidence to hold her shoulders high no matter what intimidated me. She was way more put together than anyone else I knew at our age.

While I worried about what my professors would think of my paper topics and what summer internship to pursue, Marie, business major extraordinaire, felt no fear about life after college. She viewed college as a life experience, not something to be conquered with good grades (*though she excelled in the classroom too*). Marie chose classes based on what she wanted to learn, not based on what grades she knew she could get or which friends she'd sit next to. She worked during the summer at her father's company. Her dad was grooming her to take over for him one day, if she wanted. And, during the school year, Marie signed up for internships at places such as a large national shoe company. Future employers wanted Marie to notice them, not the other way around. Marie was well on her way to greatness.

Unlike the rest of us in the women's dorm, Marie never needed anyone's approval to follow her heart—or her hobbies, either. She spent every Tuesday night repairing World War II airplanes with a group of ragtag senior citizen vets—not your typical collegiate night out. But she loved it, so it didn't matter. Even though the old men would call her "Sweetie" (which would have driven me crazy), Marie showed up faithfully every week, often with brownies or homemade candy in hand.

She left me a semester early, though, graduating with honors in December when I had another whole year of studies left. We commemorated her graduation, thanks to her parent's generosity, with a trip to Mexico. The two of us were unstoppable on the beaches of Cancun, and it was there that Marie took me to my first club and taught me how to order cocktails.

We worked well as friends because Marie never stressed over leading, while I saw the possibilities in people that she might have otherwise written off. Marie made friends with fellow tourists on our travels, while I reminded her to slow down and take a nap every now and then. Marie taught me to try new things that my ultra-conservative childhood frowned upon (besides just alcohol), while I showed her that she didn't have to isolate herself in her ambition to take on the world. Through it all, I realized I wanted to be a force of change like her too.

When Marie married Bob in 2004, she asked me to be her maid of honor, and when I married Kevin in 2007, she was mine. Proud days, I believe, for both of us.

We stayed in touch too, even with seven hundred miles separating our adult landing spots. She'd call me on her way to work in the mornings. I'd call her every time I had a crisis—no matter the hour. We'd give each other plane tickets to visit for our birthdays, as I had done with her on my thirtieth. We'd send each other cards just to say that we missed each other. We aspired one day to be those two cool grandmas at the nursing home rocking beside each other on the front porch.

We crossed many of our respective life hurdles around the same time: graduation, first jobs, marriage. Yet, when it came to motherhood, I saw us moving at a completely different pace. This was a disconnect from our previous history, and I saw the emotions of desiring to become pregnant dividing us from the start.

Marie and Bob wanted to have children for a long time before she announced, "I'm pregnant." Painful years of just trying the old-fashioned way went on and on. Fertility treatments became part of her story, just as they were part of ours. But when Marie successfully conceived without IVF in the end, I wanted to shout, "Not fair!"

But the funny thing was this: through all the years of our parallel pain, we couldn't talk about it. Any of it. And on the rare occasion when we did share, we spoke in language doctors use about our prognoses: things like "I have a cyst," or, "My cycle is too short;" or even, "I hate the nurse who works on Thursday mornings," instead of, "I *feel...*" For two women in so much similar pain, feelings were too hard to share. And when brief flashes of courage appeared, we clashed. When Marie felt like talking, I shut down. When I needed to share, Marie went straight to, "How's the weather?" I knew Marie loved me, but I wondered some days: How in the world did we used to be so close?

Yet, leaning on Sedona's lessons, I told Kevin one night before bed that I needed my girls as much as I needed him. More than ever, I needed all the love in my life, like the kind Marie offered. I vowed to try harder.

Lucy and I talked on the phone later that week. I brought up Marie and her baby-to-be. Lucy offered her usual relationship wisdom: "She probably needs you too. Talk to her. There's nothing like having your first baby to rock your world. I bet she really needs a friend right now and needs you in particular."

There's nothing like an appeal to the ego to get a person moving, is there? So I decided I would call Marie. I would break the ice. I would not let any more time pass. After all, at church I was teaching a spiritual disciplines class for Lent. The previous week's lesson had focused our attention toward hospitality. I'd invited the class to consider how God might be calling them to widen their circle of love, forgiveness, and welcome. We made a list on a white board of commitments each person hoped to make in the coming month. We prayed for God to give us the strength to follow through with the tasks on the list. Driving home that night, I couldn't help but think of Marie. I needed to be more hospitable in our friendship.

Marie and I finally spoke after a week's worth of phone tag. We started slowly. She told me about her new kitchen remodel and the bid for a new job she had just received at work. I told her about how everyone responded to my recent sermon series on characters in the Bible and how much I loved my new haircut. We trod slowly at first.

But then I just came out with it, with tears rolling down my cheeks: "I miss you so much, Marie."

"Oh, I miss you too."

To get back on the right track, I suggested that we needed to see each other face to face. We both loved traveling. So what if we met somewhere, just us for a weekend? I told Marie about a pastor's meeting I'd signed up for in North Carolina, kind of a half-way point between Virginia and Tennessee. Could we meet there? I'd even take a precious Sunday off to make it work with her schedule. Right away, Marie said yes. We'd use my hotel points and find somewhere to lay our heads near a great Mexican restaurant, the kind of food we loved to eat together. And if this hotel included an indoor pool, even better!

I sat on the plane on a Friday morning with sweaty palms and an upset stomach. I doodled happy faces in my journal trying to pump myself up. Most of all, I feared seeing her round belly. I feared something unkind coming out of my mouth. I feared my own tears in front of her and those awkward pauses of neither of us knowing what to say. But hours later in baggage claim, I put one foot in front of the other and hugged her neck while trying not to touch her stomach. Operation Weekend with Pregnant Woman was on!

The next forty-eight hours were sometimes awkward. Marie mused aloud whether her ultrasounds pictures were off limits. I didn't want to be rude, but I said no. I really wanted to say I hated how she couldn't get in the hot tub with me at the hotel or drink cocktails at happy hour. But I kept quiet. The minutes of our time together passed and we eased into conversation. I learned you can't be pouty or bitter for very long if you love a person. And Marie and I really did love each other. We loved in a

way that if we could have done anything—even the impossible—
to bring happiness to the other, we would have. In my heart I
knew she'd be a wonderful mother. That child would be lucky
to be hers! And, in a matter of months, she *could* rejoin me in
the hot tub and at happy hour. Pregnancy wasn't a sentence that
would last forever.

As I lay in bed on Saturday night, Marie fast asleep, I tried
to remember that the Hagan family journey to parenthood was
our own. Though I obviously wished ours wasn't so hard, staying
in our lane was the only way I'd get through. I could learn to
be excited about what came to me. We'd already planned to try
another round of IVF beginning in June. I tried (key word: *tried*)
to be grateful for the opportunity that this new cycle offered.
This new cycle could be our time. Weeks before, our fertility
doctor sent us to a specialist who dealt with male infertility. He
had new ideas about how we could connect quality sperm with
my eggs in the lab. These new findings raised our hopes. For our
next round of IVF, we would not be beating our heads against
the wall, for it would entail new technology.

On Sunday morning before Marie and I parted ways, I told
her this latest piece of the puzzle. To admit such a "weakness"
in front of someone so obviously in the "winning" category
felt like the definition of vulnerability to me. But I felt lighter
immediately. As the words came out of my mouth, she grabbed
me by the arm and hugged me right away. I sobbed in her arms.
"What has my life come to?" I uttered over and over again. "I
know so much about the cells of eggs and sperm!" We giggled
a little too.

Marie couldn't get me off her mind as she drove home
that day, I later learned. Over the course of the drive, a plan
formulated in her mind. As soon as she hit the front door, she
told Bob they needed to talk. They stayed up for hours chatting
about Kevin and me, carefully weighing their options.

One week later, while I sat at my desk in the church office
editing the call to worship, this zinger hit my email inbox:

Dear Elizabeth,

I love you so much and I am so heartbroken for you and Kevin. I know it is expensive and cost prohibitive and ridiculous what you are going through. I have tried to wait several days to let the grieving process have a few days to set in but I wanted to share the following. Please know this is entirely in love and caring.

Several weeks ago Bob and I were praying for you and Kevin… We feel so strongly about your situation. Bob had gotten to the point he was asking specific questions about your situation and I shared with him. He very earnestly has offered to be a sperm donor for you two. He knows that you could probably be successful with IUI [interuterian insemination], which is much cheaper, and he used the words "honored" to do it. I know that this is such an incredibly sensitive subject and has everything in the world to do with yours and Kevin's feelings and very well may not be an option for you. But I wanted you to know he would be willing to fly there on your schedule to help out and would keep it incredibly confidential. He just wondered if it might be easier if you knew the person.

I have not wanted to say anything yet as we focused our prayerful energies on Kevin, but the more walls you run into, the more it is uncomfortable not to offer. I love you very much!

Marie

What do you do after an email like this? I stared out my big bay window for the next half an hour until the church administrator's questions about boiler repairs summoned me back to life.

I knew right away that this wasn't a guilt-ridden email, a way of making up for years of less frequent conversation, or for the fact that she was pregnant and I was not. No, this was an offer from the heart of a friend who truly loved us more than there were words to say. Who knew that the carefree friendship Marie and I shared all of these years would come to this? That she'd have good sperm in her family and I wouldn't. And that she and her husband would want to give our dreams of parenthood life, literally.

Several hours later on my way home from work I called Kevin to say: "Guess what, honey, we just got offered some sperm."

"What??"

I pulled over into a gas station parking lot. "Yup, let me read you this email Marie sent this morning..." Silence came over the air waves.

How strange our journey had become! Friends offered us their sperm! *Their sperm*. I couldn't help but laugh out loud... Kevin did too. Neither of us ever thought we'd use the word "sperm" as often as household words such as *sink, chair,* or *bed*. But, what a grace-filled gift: sperm.

As I had experienced already in this journey with Kevin, Meredith, and Lucy, I now saw how profoundly Marie loved me too. Really loved me. I knew Marie and Bob would keep the whole process confidential if we accepted their offer and I became pregnant. They wanted to give this ultimate gift to us and didn't even need the credit or the parental relationship with this potential baby. But such an "I want your sperm" declaration to a best friend is not something that Kevin and I could respond to right away. The more Kevin and I talked about it, the more we realized that the best thing for us, if we ever went the route of donor sperm, was anonymous donation. Though this might provide some complicated conversations with our child as he or she grew older, we ultimately believed it would be in the best interest of any future child of ours to know only Kevin as his or her father. If we selected a donor from our friend group, someone with whom we hoped to remain in contact, awkward moments of confusion might override the security of what our loving home provided.

So, soon, I hit "reply" to that email: "Thank you so much, but we really don't think donor sperm is best for us at this time. But, wow, what a super friend you are!"

Marie graciously received our reply and confirmed what

I believed all along. Offering Bob's sperm was the only thing they could give to "fix it." "If this offer could have made your pain go away," she wrote, "It was worth any effort or personal discomfort in the long run." I understood. Everyone who felt our pain, including us, wanted to fix it. But they couldn't. We couldn't. Nothing could fix it. For our desired outcome, no amount of "Help, help, help" prayers changed things. But as much as we wanted throw up our hands and curse God, or to ask our community to do the same on our behalf, how could you curse a God who sent you friends who offered you their sperm? The offer of the sperm shocked our theology back into the steadfast hope of God being good.

Several nights later, as our normal bedtime routine unfolded, an important conversation emerged. Kevin threw our pillow shams on the floor and turned back the covers to his liking. I washed my face in our adjoining bathroom. It would be his turn to use the bathroom next. But then, with toothpaste running from the side of my mouth, I stuck my head around the corner of the open door to our room and blurted out, "Hey." Kevin knew my posture meant, "Listen." An edition of theology by Pastor Elizabeth at bedtime would soon begin.

"I've been thinking…"

"Yes," Kevin replied.

I desperately wanted to make sense of all of these failures.

"I think we have a choice here. Either we can throw everything out that we know about God, saying God is truly evil, or we can trust that God is ultimately good. And if God is good, then eventually something good is going to happen to us. This phase won't last forever."

"God is good." Kevin repeated. "This is what I want to believe too, even through all we've been through. But why is it so damn hard?"

I went on, a toothbrush hanging out of the side of my mouth all the while: "I don't know why, honey. I don't know. But as much as I want to shout to everyone I know that God is evil and doesn't care about us, that we are just getting crapped on unfairly when I know you and I didn't do anything to deserve pain like this, I just can't."

I spit out the toothpaste and wiped the white residue from the side of my lips and returned: "Call it my upbringing. Call it something I learned in seminary that stuck with me all these years. Or just call me plain stupid, but life with a hateful God just doesn't seem worth living, don't you think?"

"I get what you're saying," Kevin reassured me.

I moved toward the door threshold. "This doesn't change the fact that I feel the universe is after us…for this all seems really, really unfair. But at least if God is good there might be some hope, right?"

Kevin blurted out: "There is always hope!" Then he started to sing a silly rendition of the gospel hymn, "My hope is built on nothing less…" with the cutest smile on his face. I belly-laughed my way toward him under the covers.

As I peacefully drifted off to sleep, I felt the secure grip of this community of support. None of us knew how long we'd be in his hard place. But as we waded deeper into the mystery, God—the great Mystery—showed up for me in their faces. Kevin. Meredith. Lucy. Now Marie. Being able to name the goodness of God felt like a strong tower of refuge. But little did I know what was on its way!

10

In the Ash Heap

We took the plunge into IVF #4, hoping this would be the last time. More medication. More shots in the butt. More early morning sonograms. Even when I thought my body, mind, and soul could take no more, I gave them a talking to and made them answer, "We will." For the sake of our child-to-be, I would be a selfless vessel. I would be supermom even prior to conception. I would believe in the doctor's words about my body: "You have such a beautiful uterus. Women like you carry children successfully all the time." I would believe the odds of IVF landed in our favor.

Two Wednesday mornings after our celebratory transfer of three embryos into me (*yes, three! Go big or go home! We would deal with the triplet situation if it actually happened*), Kevin and I got in the car in the direction of our fertility clinic. The day of my pregnancy test had arrived. We'd know the results by late afternoon. I prayed for babies A, B, and C (as I had named them) as the nurse inserted the needle into my arm to draw some blood. "It's D-day," I said, hoping to stir up some emotion from the nurse. She did not look up from her task.

Was I finally pregnant? Was I pregnant with more than one? It would take till the afternoon to know something.

Kevin and I planned to be together for the news. All our dreadful experiences had formed us more into a team every day, and as a team neither one of us wanted to receive the call alone at our desks at work. My posture of "Me against the world / I don't need you, Kevin" had ended. For good or for ill, there was no doubt anymore that we were in this together. So we formulated a plan: We'd meet up at home at 2:00 p.m., the earliest possible time that the doctor would call us—a fact we now knew since this wasn't our first rodeo.

Kevin scheduled and attended back-to-back meetings through lunch time. As for me, I drove to church. I edited content for the website. I called to check on a couple of church members in the hospital. I wrote a few birthday cards. When the clock read 1:25, I packed up my computer and all my files, having no idea if I'd be in a mental state to come back to church the next day. I forgot to eat lunch.

And right on schedule, we both made it home almost exactly at 2:00 p.m. But before either of us had time to even un-tuck our dress shirts or take off our shoes, Kevin's phone rang. My heart raced as Kevin stared at the phone he'd placed on the coffee table next to where he'd just thrown his keys. Then, he picked up the phone. Looking at the caller ID, he knew who it was.

"Doctor! Doctor!"

I ran for the couch and the soft tan blanket Lucy had given me months earlier. I covered myself completely with my head buried face down. My whole body shook. The blanket muffled the sound of Kevin's conversation. I liked it this way.

Within minutes I felt the warmth of Kevin's body touching mine on the couch. I felt his hand on my back. He began to rub my back, first gently and then faster and faster. It's not good news. I knew it from his touch. He didn't have to say a word. A, B, and C were dead.

Our triplets that could have been were dead. Dead.

Kevin pulled the covers from my head, peered at my now wet cheeks and spoke words that didn't need to be said: "It didn't work. I can't believe it. The doc can't believe it either. You're not pregnant."

We didn't move. Hours passed on the clock. We'd thought we'd had bad days before, but this one now topped them all. We simply didn't know what to do with ourselves. How could this be *our* life...*again*?

By 4:00 p.m., we made our way upstairs to our bedroom, thinking maybe we could sleep the pain away. We put on our pajamas and held each other as tightly as we could under the covers. Kevin dozed off. I stared into the darkness of this very cold room on a sunny May afternoon. After Kevin woke up, we began wandering around the house in our t-shirts and fuzzy socks, sobbing almost in unison in between steps. Neither of us could pay attention to anything, so we didn't even turn on the TV or our laptops. We just sat.

I texted Meredith and Lucy about what happened. My words where simple: "We failed again." It was all I could say. I felt the shame run through all my veins. I figured I'd muster up the courage to tell Marie later. Marie felt harder to tell with *her living baby* in her belly.

In my mind, getting pregnant equaled real grown-up womanhood. I'd long felt grown up. But, still, no baby. I wanted to be a woman with children. While other women I knew desired to happily remain childless (and I celebrated that for them), I could not *not* be a mother. But this fertility stuff was not working either.

While I'd taken up residence on the couch, my phone beeped with a new message, an email from Lucy. In the hours that had passed from my sharing the news, she'd rewritten the lyrics to the hymn "Blessed Assurance." Instead of the words, "Blessed Assurance Jesus is mine. Oh what a foretaste of glory divine," and so on, this was Lucy's verse one:

> "Everything's f***** up, nothing is fine.
>
> Keep getting screwed over all of the time.
>
> Shit after shit keeps hitting the fan.
>
> If this is God's doing, what a f***** up plan.
>
> This is my story, this is my song— This is so really effing wrong!
>
> This is my story, this is my song— This is so really effing wrong!"

It was sacrilegious, of course, and maybe would have offended some members of my church, but it proved the best balm for my angry soul. I wrote her back: "Your email = the best part of my day."

Sometime later, Meredith stood at our front door, knocking still dressed up from work in a form-fitting black suit and high heels. What a shock for her to just show up! I let her in. She told us she'd left work as soon as she could: "I just needed to come and see you both. I can't believe it didn't work! I can't believe it!" She bore the despondent look of our failure all over her face. And immediately she plopped in between Kevin and me on the couch. Tentatively she inched closer in my direction but I would have nothing of her care. I soon got up and walked to the other side of the room, starting to pace around the room again. Rage enveloped my bones, so forceful that not even Meredith—my beloved Meredith—could do anything about it. While I didn't want to hurt her feelings, I also hoped she'd leave soon. When she left, I am embarrassed to say that I didn't even thank her for coming. But there were no words. I needed space. I was afraid of what I might say or do.

About dinnertime, Kevin offered a brilliant plan: "Let's get drunk."

"That sounds like a great idea." I fired back. "And I want to eat cheese. Buckets and buckets of cheese."

I'd given up cheese for months now. The acupuncturist I'd seen along with the fertility doctor this go-round told me to lay off dairy in preparation for the procedure. I'd obediently followed. But, what a scam! What a complete scam. I loved cheese. All that suffering for nothing.

Kevin and I piled in his car—me in my yoga pants and long sleeved youth group t-shirt, Kevin in his jeans and a lightweight pull over sweater—and headed to a Mexican restaurant a couple miles from our house. I couldn't wait to tell the waitress, "I want a bowl of *queso*." Kevin ordered a beer. And another beer. I ordered the strongest margarita offered. We swore in between bites of chips, staring into one another's droopy eyes, waiting until one of us was sober enough to drive home. I left the restaurant a few pounds heavier I'm sure, but no less in pain. Silence engulfed our car.

Waking the next morning with a horrible headache, I made the delirious decision to go to church. I felt I needed to keep something that felt normal in my life. Too bad I was in the helping profession, though! What shape was I in to help anyone? Still, I didn't want to start asking for time off. Who knew how long this painful time would go on? I might *really* need time off later.

Kevin told me he'd hoped I'd stay home, but proposed a compromise: "Stay two hours. Let them see your face, then come home and hibernate."

I growled when he said "hibernate." I was tired of hibernating—hadn't I been doing this routine long enough?

In his own way, Kevin dutifully went to work. One of his staff had recently received a life-altering diagnosis, meaning everything about his team needed to be reorganized. His CEO had promised the board a paper for review at the end of the week and needed Kevin's input, and a marketing project on which he'd taken the lead hung in the balance. Kevin was a master at turning his emotions off when it came to work. Me, not so much.

I fought back tears for two hours at my desk, hoping maybe someone might hug me without asking questions. But, after shuffling the papers alone, I drove home in the same fog in which I'd arrived and curled up with the blinds down in our home office in my big, green sermon-writing chair. I wrapped myself in a blanket and turned on the computer. My plan for making it to nightfall included only one thing: *West Wing*. Lots and lots of *West Wing*. What could be better than some Josiah Bartlet and Josh Lyman in my life? Friends of mine raved about the show, but I'd never seen an episode. I decided to drown myself in TV, which didn't involve either contact with another person or conversation about my body.

In the days that followed, I continued the pattern, gradually adding more hours at work to my day. But, when I hit the front door in the afternoon, it was all about my pajamas, a ponytail on top of my head, and *West Wing*.

I deemed 4:30 p.m. happy hour and made myself a vodka cranberry every day. I only drank one, fearing that if I started drinking more, it might become a problem. I talked to no one except church staff or parishioners in crisis and Kevin. I ignored Lucy's calls and Meredith's texts. Marie required no attention, as she joyfully planned her upcoming shower for her baby girl. Everything I knew and trusted had failed me; what was there really to say? Though I'd learned that my sister friends could be trusted, I didn't know how to let anyone in with *this* kind of pain. I just did not know.

When I got tired of *West Wing*, I'd put on a jacket over my t-shirt and flannel pants, sit in the dirt of our side yard, and pick up rocks. We'd always wanted to repave our driveway, and clearing the rocks was something we knew we'd have to do first. I liked getting projects done. My previous congregation even affectionately labeled me the "Task Master." This mindless activity seemed like the perfect time-passer to me. So I sat in the dirt.

After a week without speaking (*a complete aberration for us*), Lucy emailed me with some direct words. I guess she didn't like my zero-communication plan. She told me of how her heart ached for our loss, but that I couldn't keep going on like this. "You need me, and I really need you too. I miss you. You aren't allowed to ignore me for this long!" She went on to ask: "How can I be in your life? I want to know!"

Many months before, Lucy had gone through a crisis of her own. A dear aunt of hers had died, an aunt that was more like a mother than an aunt. She'd called me right away. I cried big tears with her, driving many miles to reach her town at the time, sitting with her, inspecting her refrigerator, and bringing food to her to make sure she was eating. I didn't think twice about doing it. But to receive in return an insistent, "How can I be in your life?" was not what I expected. Her concern startled me awake. I would respond to her. I just didn't know what to say.

After a couple of more episodes of *West Wing*, I got some ideas. If Lucy really wanted to be in my life, then I would bluntly tell her how:

1. Come pick up rocks with me in the yard.
2. Read to me the book of Job.
3. Call Mary (our mutual friend who had recently lost her pre-school aged son to cancer). Tell her what I am going through. It will make me feel better if she knows.

Deep down I hoped she'd follow my requests, but I imagined I might be too demanding even for her. Classic case of my pushing away what I wanted the most: love.

Lucy responded to my email right away. "I'm so glad to hear from you. Of course I can do those things. When do you want me to come over?"

I was shocked! We set up a time during one of my "happy hours."

A couple days later, Lucy came for *West Wing* and cocktails. After one episode, we moved outside and dug more rocks out of the dirt. The mosquitoes really started biting our ankles so we didn't make it long outside. Then, Lucy plopped down on our couch and, like the patriarch of the family on Christmas Eve, I presented her my Bible. Even if I didn't have the strength to murmur anything, Lucy knew what to do. She opened to Job, chapter one, and began reading:

There was once a man in the land of Uz whose name was Job. That man was blameless and upright, one who feared God and turned away from evil. There were born to him seven sons and three daughters… One day when his sons and daughters were eating and drinking wine in the eldest brother's house, a messenger came to Job and said, "The oxen were plowing and the donkeys were feeding beside them, and the Sabeans fell on them and carried them off, and killed the servants with the edge of the sword; I alone have escaped to tell you." While he was still speaking, another came and said, "The fire of God fell from heaven and burned up the sheep and the servants, and consumed them; I alone have escaped to tell you… (Job 1:1–2, 13–16)

How I got the idea for Lucy to read Job to me I don't know, other than the fact that it's the one book in scripture where you can definitively say somebody faithful endured suffering upon suffering. I felt both faithful and screwed. Job was my new homeboy and I wanted to understand him more. Though I'd read, taught on, and even attempted to preach on the whole story of Job once for my very first sermon in seminary (*yes, the whole thing*), I gasped as I heard the story read in Lucy's voice. Job came near to me in his ash heap.

After finishing chapter 1, Lucy skipped over to the part featuring Job's friends in chapter 5 and following. I listened to each of Job's friends trying to make meaning out of his losses by believing this whole mess was somehow about unconfessed sin. I thought about all the times the question "What had I done wrong?" had crossed my mind, wondering whether all our infertility and fertility failures were somehow our fault. Did we bring this on ourselves? Could we make this horrible season end by reconciling something that was amiss in our lives? However, every time temptation led me there, I remembered that I believed in a God of blessings, not curses. Kevin and I did not make this happen to us. It just *was*. But why was God so cruel to Job? Why was God so quiet? What hell Job must have been in not to hear God's voice for all those chapters. And then, how could his friends say such mean things? I kept thinking about how Job needed a really good pastor in his life. Lucy was not like Job's friends at all.

Lucy, with her flowing blonde locks and blue eyes, is the kind of person you want to be your pastor. Not only is she warm from the moment you meet her, but she's calm, levelheaded, and waits for the right time to say what's on her mind. She's got that look that reflects back, "I've got all the time in the world for you." She's not afraid to grab your hand or put your head on her shoulder when the situation calls for it. Parishioners love her for this.

But, on this day, in my ash heap, Lucy was not a pastor or a colleague or even just someone that I went to seminary with. Lucy was *my* sister friend—the kind of friend I could not push away even if I tried. Lucy knew me too well. She didn't leave for the afternoon till I ate something substantial. (I was a lightweight drinker, after all.) And cereal didn't count! We set a time for her to come over again soon, something of a glimmer of happiness to mark on my calendar.

The following Saturday afternoon, well into season two of *West Wing*, I turned off the computer. I took my place back in the rocks alone. I sent Kevin to the grocery store for food for the church potluck I'd put him in charge of the next day. The church ladies liked his cooking better than mine anyway. He shouldn't have been home for hours when he startled me by pulling up in the driveway. His car stopped less a foot from my rock pile. As he emerged from the car, Kevin held a bouquet of sunflowers with full stems. I'd never seen such large flowers that weren't in a pot. I couldn't believe he got such flowers from anywhere near our house *(or maybe he didn't?)*. He leaned down, put a hand on my dusty back, and kissed me on the cheek. I snapped at him, asking why he was home so quickly, not even thanking him for the flowers. My mind could not internalize the beauty of them. Nor could it give up any of my precious alone time, time where I was not responsible for anyone's feelings except my own.

"The store didn't have exactly what I needed for the potluck, so I decided to come home and make something up with what's in the freezer." Kevin paused. I barely looked at him.

"Don't you want to come in and help me?"

"Nope, I'm perfectly content in the dirt."

"Well, suit yourself then." Kevin shut the door hard from frustration with his mopey wife as he went to the kitchen. My mind felt numb. All the friends I wanted were rocks.

Soon, persistent Kevin came back outside. He would not leave me alone. He smiled at me in his silliest face that said, "I love you and I'm not leaving you out here any longer." I could not resist *that* face—the face I'd fallen in love with six years earlier. Okay, I guess I could sit at the table if he did all the work. Kevin started pulling out every pot and pan in our small galley kitchen. Cooking oil, spices, and flour lined our counters. Normally I would have fussed over what a mess he was making or clean up behind him, but it didn't seem all that important given the ash heap I had just come from. Within an hour he presented two chicken pot pies: one for us to eat for supper, and one for the church folks the next day. When I didn't want to take more than a couple of bites, he offered to feed me. With his spoon in my mouth, I ate.

The intimacy of the meal gave me strength to text Meredith for the first time in two weeks. Like Lucy, I knew I couldn't be silent forever toward her. And this is how it started:

"I wish getting drunk made things better. I think it only makes it worse."

She wrote me back immediately. "I know, my dear. I know."

I kept going from one day to the next because of those willing to embrace my ash heap.

11

Resurrection in the Kitchen

In many ways, I grew up in an ash heap—the emotional kind. In the community of my childhood, we didn't talk about our emotions or our pain or what made us most afraid or excited. We didn't sit around and talk about big ideas for changing the world. We simply talked about things that got us from point A to point B in a day. "Sign up for the church ski retreat over winter break." "What time is your dance lesson over?" and "Dinner starts at 6:00 p.m.," are the conversations I remember the most.

I found a refuge of realness from time to time in church youth group or at school with a teacher or two. These folks would ask me questions beyond my plans for summer vacation or SAT scores and actually stick around to listen to what I said. My greatest refuge, hands down, was Mrs. Cartwright's classroom at my conservative Christian high school. I sat in Mrs. Cartwright's ninth, tenth, and twelfth grade Bible classes lapping up anything I could glean from her lessons. Her intelligence and passion made even the reluctant students want to learn because all her students knew she cared about each one of them. She's still the only female Bible teacher my high school has ever endorsed.

I loved Mrs. Cartwright because she was insightfully attentive to things others simply overlooked about me, especially when she wrote comments on my homework assignments—one of the best gifts a socially awkward teenager could receive. Mrs. Cartwright even took me aside my senior year of high school with a direct word: "God has great plans for you in your life. You are going to do amazing things. I can't wait to see what happens!" After graduation, I held her words close. I said them over and over in my head. As long as I could remember them, I believed our connection would remain.

After high school, Mrs. Cartwright insisted I call her by her first name—Jean—and we kept in touch, at least as much as a teacher and former student could. My freshman year in college, I stopped by her classroom during Christmas break just to say hi. I sent her an email with an update every now and then. I didn't want her to fade away. I think she loved me too, as much as I had allowed her to know me. But that was that. Our separate paths called us. Jean, to me, felt like one big missed opportunity in the world of adult friendship.

Meanwhile, back in our house, our baby making plans in early 2012 centered upon IUI (interuterian insemination) with anonymous donor sperm. We'd both gotten to the point of exhaustion with our own bodies, and Kevin wanted to give donor sperm a try. If you'd have asked us years before if we'd ever be here, we'd have told you, "Hell, no!" But, our guiding principle in all things fertility related became: God can make families in all sorts of ways. Who says that God could not give us the child that was meant to be ours through the gracious donation of life from another person? Painstakingly, we began poring over sperm donors from a bank in California. We found a young match who we felt like would be a perfect baby daddy (at least from what his paperwork told us about him). Donor # 56878 felt a lot like Kevin: outgoing, sensitive, and wanting to use his life to help address the big problems of the world. And, as a bonus, they shared the same blood type too.

Sadly, rounds one and two of IUI failed. Then we tried round three. Again my period came like clockwork. Our scorecard included now not one but seven failed fertility treatments. *Really?* How was *this* my life? How much more grief could I take? Meredith, Lucy, and Marie reminded me of how strong I was. But the word *strong* felt like a crappy way of predicting that this whole saga would never end. I wanted to trade in my "strong" card for a weak one if it meant that I could finally be pregnant!

However, the church, as always, gave my mind opportunities to think about something else. My yellow legal pad to-do list read "Find a retreat leader" for the spiritual gifts seminar I planned for late January. I wanted to bring alive the season of Epiphany in the liturgical calendar that most members did not understand. I wanted the church folks to consider anew how God might be calling them to serve others. I wanted us to do something fun as a congregation. The line item in the education section of the budget showed enough funds to bring in a guest speaker.

Jean came to mind right way as the perfect fit for this special project. In the tenth grade, she'd taught a semester-long unit entirely on spiritual gifts. Not only did her leadership help me fall in love with the concept of all Christians receiving special gifts, but I loved taking the inventory she provided to uncover mine: exhortation and leadership. These affirmations of my giftedness gave awkward fifteen-year-old me confidence and clarity like nothing else had. In fact, ever since then I'd kept my notes from tenth grade with my other books and papers, pulling them out every now and then to remember how much I'd learned. I believed Jean's teaching could inspire my congregation just as it had me so many years before.

I tracked down her phone number and she said yes right away! And, with fertility loss seven still fresh, what a perfect distraction (*or opportunity?*) to have a visit from Jean on my professional and personal calendar. I offered to get her a hotel room but she said, "No, let me stay at your house." Corresponding with her through email in the weeks leading up to the retreat brought back to the forefront of my mind the sweetness that I treasured about her. "I can't wait to spend time with you again," she wrote several times, "and to meet your church."

On an unusually warm January afternoon, Kevin and I picked her up at the airport. My head filled with lots of anxiety over seeing her again after so long. Who invites her high school teacher to fly in for the weekend? Apparently, I did. But deep down the possibilities filled me with joy. Jean Cartwright in my house! How cool!

When we arrived back at our place, Kevin scurried away to finish something at work. I told Jean I needed to make chili for the cook-off that would be part of the retreat supper and headed straight for the kitchen. I thought she would just relax or watch TV in the living room while I cooked, or maybe look over her notes for the evening. But after rolling her suitcase into our guest room, I heard her say: "Hey, why don't you let me chop the onions? Oh, I can cut the peppers too!"

"Are you sure you want to help?" I asked doubtfully, thinking I was a terrible host.

Jean answered by tucking her short blonde hair behind her ears and rolling up the sleeves of her bright blue sweater.

"I'm not one to sit around, Elizabeth. Of course I can help. I'm glad just to be with you." *Glad just to be with me?* This got my attention!

Side-by-side in my kitchen I was no longer alone in my thoughts about all the "what ifs." We began talking as if no time had passed since we were last together. She shared about changes to my hometown, describing the fun new restaurants and places where the kids hung out. She told me what she knew about the lives of students of hers that were former classmates of mine. The time passed quickly as we couldn't stop talking, and our fabulous chili came swiftly together.

At the retreat, my congregation took to Jean's teaching right away. Many couldn't take their eyes off her. It thrilled my pastor's heart to hear folks say, "My gift is leadership," or, "I never knew that prophecy could be so important in the church."

The next morning, I woke up around eight and stumbled toward the refrigerator only to find Jean bright-eyed and already on her second cup of coffee. Though it took a bowl of Raisin Bran and some orange juice before I could be verbal, Jean quickly declared, "I want to hear more about you." I wiped the sleep fully from my eyes. I wrapped my favorite blanket around me and lodged myself in between the oversized pillows of my tan couch facing her. I was glad neither of us needed to hurry. Kevin, exhausted from a long week of work, would not wake up for several hours.

How was I? Being a woman in her thirties without children felt awful. Having my life dictated by the fertility calendar felt agonizing. Handing over control of my body to doctors I didn't really believe cared about me felt cruel. Soon the unexpected floodgates of our reproductive pain opened in the safety of her presence. I told her all about the worst doctors and nurses we'd met along the way. I told her about my agony two Christmases ago preaching on Christmas Eve when our IVF had just failed. "I couldn't stand to look at that baby doll in the manager on the altar!" I told her about Kevin's struggles with my sadness, not knowing how to fix me, and the day we'd almost used the *"d"* word about our marriage, many months before. In some of our worst moments, Kevin thought I might want a baby more than I wanted to be his wife. Jean and I consumed a box of Kleenex. Honoring the spirit of my openness, she began telling me more about some of her deepest life pains. Not only was Jean in *my* house, but we were talking, really talking. Wow.

By the afternoon, I felt even more grateful that I had not over-planned the weekend with church activities. I needed Jean as much as the church did. We had a lot of ground to cover with one another. We moved through it as we took in the sights of downtown Washington, D.C. She hadn't been to D.C. in ages, and I'd promised to show her whatever she wanted. On our leisurely stroll around the Lincoln Memorial and the Washington Monument, we discussed deep life questions, such as: "What made you feel most alive in high school?" "Who are your best friends?" and, "What do you love most about your husband?" As we both answered, I knew I was walking alongside a kindred spirit. "You really don't like going to social events without a purpose, Jean? You don't like leaving the house in the morning until you've spent some time writing? You don't like spending money frivolously?"

"Me either!" I exclaimed. Was I dreaming or was she real? This dear one whom I'd always loved from afar was more like me than I'd ever realized. Jean carried herself with such determination as she walked. I could feel her confidence with every step. Jean really wanted to use her life to help others find their deepest joys. I did too. It was one of the many reasons I'd accepted my ordination vows several years before.

In the evening, Kevin and I planned to welcome some friends over for dinner. I really wanted Lucy to meet Jean, especially. And Jean volunteered again.

"Want me to cut up the apples for the pie?"

"Yeah, that would be great. I suck at cutting."

Jean chopped fast. Before I knew it, my pie pan overflowed with the neatest chopped apples I'd ever seen. I glanced over at her while rolling out the piecrust. Her eyes sparkled with the delight; I suspected mine showed too. Something deeper was connecting us, and we both knew it. I was in awe of her beauty. This amazing woman was chopping my apples in my kitchen. Soon, with the pie baking in the oven, I told her, "Our kitchen hasn't smelled this good in months!" It had been a long time since we'd had much energy to cook.

And, later that evening, Jean followed behind Kevin as he prepared the main meal (roasted pork with a Brussels sprout hash and a side of mashed potatoes), washing the dishes. I'd never seen our countertops so clean! Our rhythm together felt as if she'd been a frequent visitor in our home countless times before. Kevin whispered to me later, "I really like her. What a sweet friend!" And the rest of our gang loved her too.

The next morning, up early again, Jean surprised us. Before we had time to object, a prepared hot breakfast lay before our eyes. From the meager rations left in the refrigerator, she found enough for French toast, bacon, and a fruit salad. I couldn't believe it. It was the most colorful breakfast plate I'd seen in my house in years, complete with folded cloth napkins I guess she found in our linen closet. As we sat down, Jean offered us coffee and tea, pouring cups of what we wanted and showing us the cream and syrup already on the table. We lapped up the deliciousness while I proofread the sermon to be delivered in a couple of hours. I felt no obligation to chat it up with her. She knew I needed to study. Kevin and Jean let me be. When I looked up from the page several times in her direction, Jean's smile beamed with pride. She'd told me on her walk the day before, "I can't wait to hear one of my favorite students preach!" Though Kevin and I held the role of hosts, the woman in charge obviously was Jean. We just needed to get out of the way! And, for Jean, being in charge meant showing me what it was like to eat real food again. For, eating is a holy act, soul- and- mind-filled work that would take time for which to prepare. If Kevin and I were to eat, really eat again, it would require the use of pots and pans. It would require standing on the rug in front of the sink with hands on plates. It would require loading the dishwasher regularly. All just as she had done. My norm of microwave popcorn for lunch and take-out cheeseburgers for dinner wasn't going to cut it anymore! To have energy for physical, spiritual, or emotional birth, I would need to rejoin the rhythm of my own kitchen. Jean's example made this very clear!

After teaching one more lesson at church and our worship service followed by lunch, we headed home so Jean could pack. As I sat on our guest bed while she neatly organized her clothes, she worked in one last lesson. Jean wanted me to remember Kevin's pain, Kevin's perspective, and Kevin's needs too. "You aren't the only one hurting here. Be good to your husband. You've got something good going on with him." She added some direct language about setting aside quality time with him that night after we dropped her off. "Please take care of each other."

It was tempting to smart back with, "Yes, Mrs. Cartwright." But I didn't.

In love, Jean offered spot-on advice. To make it out of this dark cloud I needed to plant myself firmly on Kevin's support team, just as he had done for me. I heard these words because *Jean* said them. Kevin would want to call her months later to say thank you.

Being a delayed processor, it took me a while to sort out the deeper meaning of this fun weekend. When Jean left, I felt really different, though I couldn't name how. Jean blessed our kitchen and taught my church well, for sure, but there was more.

A couple of weeks later, around 11:00 p.m., I turned over in bed with sudden insight. We'd turned off the lights thirty minutes earlier and I knew Kevin was asleep. But I made some noise on my side of the bed and I startled him awake anyway with a loud cough. I feared if I didn't say what I knew I might not ever say it. He barely rolled over when I charged in:

"I've been thinking, trying to figure out what was so amazing about last weekend beside the obvious of reconnecting with a friend I loved."

Rubbing his eyes, Kevin asked: "Well, what is it?" With tears streaming down my face full of the kind of emotion that only a major life revelation could hold, I said, "This is what I know. I've always wanted someone nurturing in my life who saw me the way Jean does. I have a hard time saying this aloud, but it's true."

"Yes," Kevin said as he reached over, putting his arm on my shoulder and pulling me closer to his side of the bed, "and?"

"Then, Jean showed up. And I was blown away! She was more amazing than I ever imagined."

I took a breath and went on as Kevin grabbed my hand for support. I think he had some idea of what was coming. "I'm thirty-two, for goodness sake. And married! This shouldn't be happening now. I should be having a baby right now, not working on myself. Or being mothered." I started talking faster: "But I believe Jean's coming to visit and her presence back in my life was God's way of saying to me, 'I know you. I know what you most need, even if you're too scared to ask for it.'"

In my mind I was connecting the dots back to that day in Sedona when the therapist told me I was holding back some of the deepest expressions of myself. I realized Jean's coming was the opportunity to put this new way of life in actual practice. I needed to be in relationship with women like her. I needed to ask for more of what I wanted.

"Wow. That's amazing, Elizabeth!" Kevin offered. In response, I wrapped my arms around him and buried my head in his chest. Looking through the dark toward his face I said, "Yeah, isn't it? Really amazing!"

"Kind of like resurrection?"

"Yes! Perfect word. Kind of like resurrection." I sat up in bed facing him, stunned by what we'd named together. "I'm so proud of how theological you just sounded, honey. I've trained you so well!" We laughed, a rarity when such tender subjects appeared on the discussion docket.

I'm sure the word *resurrection* came to Kevin's mind because he remembered all too well my rant the previous Easter. With my head buried so deeply in the pit of our pain, I couldn't find a hopeful thing to say for my big "Super Bowl of sermons" day. "I can't talk about resurrection this year. Where's ours?" I kept repeating over and over. The only way I pulled off a sermon titled, "Resurrection for All of Us" came because I called every colleague I knew to ask them about what they intended to preach and wrapped my head around my most hopeful thoughts even as doubt ran straight through them.

Yet, in this resurrection moment, I simply rejoiced. God had brought a wise mentor back into my life, something I'd always wanted. Lying back against Kevin, soon I started crying again as I thought more about what I'd just declared: "This is what love feels like, I think—God's love! God must really love me, Kevin. God must really, really love me! Resurrection is such a wonderful thing."

My litany of happiness went on and on as I took in this great known, yet unknowable, thing. Poor Kevin stayed awake to hear every word. Finally, I let him off the hook and told my exhausted husband goodnight. But I couldn't sleep. Of course, I hoped Jean and I would stay friends and have more adventures together, but this was about more than just her. God loved me: how deeply this knowledge now registered in my soul. I believed God had sent Jean to remind me.

The next morning on the way to work, resurrection reverberated over the tan seats of my Chevy sedan. I found the most happy-clappy church CD I could find stuffed in my car's glove compartment. It took a long time to dig out an appropriate one since when I was depressed I listened only to hard rock. With each note I belted out, I felt my spiritual muscles stretching in belief. God *really* did love *me*. And God loving me meant some practical changes:

Less take-out dinner every night—I was ready to cook again. Resurrection was coming to our kitchen.

Less fear of "being too much." I *could* learn to pursue deeper relationships with people I loved, such as Jean. Resurrection was coming to my day planner.

Less criticizing the best parts of myself. I *was* the woman I'd loved so much in Jean. Resurrection was coming to my core.

Sure, insecurities and relapses would come, but resurrection was indeed God's most perfect gift.

When I walked into my spiritual director's office two weeks later, she told me she hardly recognized me. "Your whole demeanor has shifted since I last saw you. You look so light and free."

I told her, "I think I just encountered God as Mother."

We unpacked the statement for the next hour, with no grand revelations on the Divine Feminine other than affirming together that infertility did not leave me unseen by God. I needed Mother-God, and Mother-God was with me. We claimed that my dreams, my big dreams for my life did not need to end. It was really okay to be honest about my desires. And nurture from other wise ones topped that list.

Around the house, Kevin loved that I couldn't stop kissing him and volunteering to make dinner. Our kitchen counters became one of the happiest spaces I touched every day. And Jean and I started talking on the phone almost every week.

12

Maybe We Should Feed the Children?

Who would have imagined that it was work—that thing Kevin and I poured ourselves into while waiting for parenthood to come—that would be *the* thing that would propel us toward a new reality of parenthood altogether? But it was.

A month after Jean's visit, on a Monday night around seven o'clock, Kevin phoned me (as was his custom) to say he'd be home shortly. Before he could say a word more, I asked, "Do you want Brussels sprouts or okra with the lemon chicken in the oven?"

"Oh, it doesn't matter what we have," Kevin replied quickly.

"Okay," I said as I stood over the bottom freezer drawer. Executive decision made: we'd go with Brussels sprouts, my favorite. I would steam them and wait for Kevin to get home to do the rest. He's the spice man in our household, making my otherwise standard meals full of zest.

Kevin continued to speak: "I have something to tell you. I got an interesting phone call today."

"Oh, what?" I said, as I half paid attention. The chicken was just a little too pink in the center. It would need a little more time in the oven. I set the timer on the microwave above the stove for five more minutes.

With these cooking decisions made, I took a deep breath, plopping down on the couch in the adjoining room. I imagined he would offer an update about another friend of ours pregnant or some news about a family member suddenly ill (the kind of calls I dreaded receiving). But, instead, he proclaimed, "A recruiter called and wants me to apply for the position of President and CEO of Feed the Children."

Jarred back to the reality by Kevin's words I exclaimed, "What? Oh my God. That's crazy. How did they get your name?"

"I think they're pursuing candidates who are currently CEOs or COOs at large nonprofits. My name just made the list."

"Isn't that a big organization that feeds kids in Africa?"

"Yeah, it's one of those."

"Oh, wow, honey, that's big!"

"Yeah, it is. But there's one catch."

"What?"

"Its headquarters is in Oklahoma."

Oklahoma? Suddenly, visions of cowboys, flatlands, and red state conservative politics filled my head. I'd visited the state once when I was in college, and the highlight of the trip was a dirt bike race. I wasn't so sure I ever needed to return. When I left Alabama to go to seminary in the "northern state" of North Carolina (literally, that's what people in the Deep South called it), I was done with all things Bible Belt. I vowed never to go back to any place where Southern Baptists, Republican governors, and "Jesus Saves" bumper stickers were the norm.

I fired back at Kevin: "Oklahoma? Hell no… I mean, that's great and all, but Oklahoma? We could never live in Oklahoma. Don't they know what I do for a living?"

It's true: most Baptist churches in the Bible Belt do not like women preachers, especially *progressive* women preachers. This was a simple fact. Being a preacher, a preacher with my own church, was so important to my identity. Even if I was a thirty-something woman sans child, the church gave me meaningful things to do with my time.

Yet, as Kevin relayed more about the opportunity, I could tell by the speed of his speech that he was excited. He'd always dreamed about leading a big organization. Leadership was his spiritual gift to the core, as we'd just studied in Jean's class. I didn't want to be *that* wife who said no. He needed to call the recruiter back. What could it hurt?

"Well, honey, it's going to be interesting to see how this all ends up," I offered later as we took the first bites of our dinner.

After one in-person meeting with the recruiter's office at the end of the week, the game changed. Kevin's unique background met all the qualifications. He offered every quality they were looking for, even at age thirty-nine. His diverse array of previous experiences in the government, private, and nonprofit sectors wowed the search firm. "We want to present you to the board as one of our final candidates. We think you are perfect for us and us for you. You've just powered your way to the top of our list."

"Oh, damn," was my first reaction to this news. Maybe we really did have to think about this. "*Ok-la-homa*," the musical number made famous by Rodgers and Hammerstein, kept running through my head.

The next steps in the search process included several other phone conversations and eventually a visit to Oklahoma City, where Kevin met the board and executive team for the first time. It was as if the heavens were opening and illuminating a very clear path. We could hardly keep up. Nor could our friends. Lucy looked afraid when I told her how excited this opportunity made Kevin. "Oh, I don't know what I would do without you here," she kept saying. But, as much as things seemed to fall into place, the two of us weren't sure what we would do if he were offered the position. How could we say yes to Oklahoma? "We'd both need to be all in," Kevin told me numerous times. "I won't take this job if you aren't feeling it too." But how did I feel? I wasn't sure.

"God, you are really, really funny," I muttered one night in my prayers. Could it be any more ironic? Kevin's potential big professional break was coming at an organization devoted to feeding children. We couldn't have any children of our own, as hard as we tried, but we were going to be asked to feed everybody else's children? Sigh. Deep, deep sigh. Maybe it wasn't the nicest thought, but infertility brought out the snark in me.

We needed to consider a lot more than geography. If Kevin took this job, he would immediately step into a role as a more prominent national public figure. By nature of being his wife, my life would become more public too—especially in the context. For some people, this might be scary or unwanted attention, but for me with big dreams of being an influencer on a stage beyond the church I pastored (*because, slowly, I was starting to believe in my own voice*), maybe this new calling was for me too. Over the last several months, in fact, I had found myself daydreaming of living out a more nontraditional ministry anyway, writing and speaking on behalf of a cause I really believed in. Feed the Children could be just this! With quickness that surprised us, we both began voicing how, if he became this organization's president, we could draw upon our diverse contacts to get others excited about this great mission of feeding hungry kids too.

But, back at the church, I was busy preaching a sermon series on Moses' relationship to the grumbling children of Israel in the desert. I loved preaching because, as I studied the texts, I often worked through my own discernment process. Insights for me emerged just as I was seeking insights for the congregation. This sermon series would be no different, as I most certainly had Feed the Children on the brain.

On a cold winter day, trying to be creative or at least hold the attention of the congregation, I instructed the ushers to hand out rocks to attendees. I made some silly joke during the announcement time about not throwing the rocks at me if they didn't like what I said, and invited everyone to hold on to their rocks for further instruction at the end of the sermon.

When it came time for me to climb the four stairs that led to the raised pulpit, I took my standard Sunday morning deep breath and opened in prayer. I spoke about the wilderness wanderings and how the children of Israel could find no water and demanded that the Lord provide. I told them about how Moses, bewildered and confused, asked the Lord what he should do. God instructed him to go and stand before the people and strike a rock. Though the rock was old, new streams would come from it, the Lord said. Moses hit the rock as instructed, and water came.

I reminded everyone about the rocks in their hands and then looked as many of parishioners in the eyes as I could and said: "Rub this rock, feel it smoothness. Put your fingertips in its cracks. Notice its color. Imagine its coming to be in the earth, holding up the foundations. Think about the story you've heard proclaimed and consider how God might want to resurrect your hopes, your needs from places in your life you once thought were long dead or buried. This is the good news today: water can come from even the deadest of springs."

Later, I encouraged everyone to take the rocks with them in the coming week to remember the story.

Every Sunday after church, I asked Kevin: "What did you think of my sermon?" Sometimes I'd later wish I hadn't, for Kevin could be painfully honest. On this day, I thought I had preached a good (or least decent) sermon and was looking forward to moving on to my Sunday afternoon nap. But Kevin belted out a response before I had time to ask him any questions: "I had an experience with God in church today."

What!?

This was not normal Kevin-speak. His own relationship with God was much more private than mine. Neither being married to a pastor nor all our years of wrestling deeply with infertility had changed that about him. It was a special occasion if he brought up God. Yet, as he looked over at me, I noticed the coloring in his face had washed out, the way it does when he's been thinking seriously. I was glad to be buckled into my seat for this narration. Who knew what I was about to hear?

"Well, tell me about it."

Kevin proceeded to give me a play-by-play of the service from his pew. How during the five minutes of silent meditation time we observed every Sunday, he prayed asking God to help him know about what to do. Was Feed the Children God's plan for our family? Or was it just his ego getting in the way? The more he prayed, he said, the more he felt like the Spirit said, "Listen!"

"I know this sounds crazy, Elizabeth."

Looking over at Kevin in the driver's seat when we stopped at a red light, I met his eyes: "It's okay. I get it. I'm a pastor, remember?"

"Yeah. Okay… I think there are only two other times in my life when I felt God speak to me directly like God did today."

"Oh? When?"

"Once when I said yes to becoming a Christian and being baptized at age twelve, and then again when I was trying to figure out if it was right for me to marry you."

"Really?"

"Yeah, I've told you that. When I sat in Duke Chapel during your graduation and asked God if you were really the one for me, it was a very clear YES!"

Beaming with delight at his sharing this story I'd actually never heard before, I nudged him on: "Well, what about today?"

"As I prayed and prayed during the meditation time, and then as I held on to that rock at the end of your sermon, God seemed to keep saying to me, 'Go feed my children. I need you to feed my children. And then you'll have your own.' And with these words, I can't describe it, Elizabeth, but a peace came over me. And I know I will get this job, and when I do, I will have to accept it."

Stunned, we both sat in silence for a while. The moment felt holy, as only the budding of a new calling can.

Later on I confided in him that I'd been thinking about the organization too during the sermon-writing process—that maybe this opportunity would be a tool that was a part of a greater plan we couldn't even conceive right now. And, because of this, I just needed to stop rolling my eyes every time the word *Oklahoma* came up.

I gave Kevin my blessing to pursue the process with gusto.

Several weeks later, Kevin traveled alone for one more meeting with the board in Oklahoma City. He reported to me about how they said he wowed them with his first 180-day plan.

Afterward, Kevin called me in tears from the hotel room. I'd never heard him so weepy before.

"I don't know what it is or how it is that you deal with so much emotion in your day-to-day job, but I came back to the room and couldn't stop crying. I have to say that I really like this organization and these people. I really want this job."

Terror and glee ran through my veins at the same time. Was this really happening to us? Something good after so much disappointment? Something *this* big?

We didn't have to wait long to figure it out. A short time later, it was official. Kevin was the only one the board would consider for the final vote. When it came down to it, the board was unanimous. The board of directors asked Kevin to lead the team. My love or lack of love for Oklahoma notwithstanding, God said, "Go!" and we needed to go. I hoped the details of my unique role and contributions would become clearer in due time. I believed they would. I'd figure out how/when to end my relationship with my beloved church in the next couple of months.

With our Sunday best in tow, Kevin and I made our way to Oklahoma City to declare to the world that Feed the Children had called our family to serve. On April 4, 2012, the headline on the front page of *The Oklahoman* was: "Feed the Children Names Kevin Hagan New President and CEO." Kevin's picture was positioned to the right. I would not be employed with the organization, but this was not the kind of job that Kevin could do without me by his side. If we'd had learned anything from our years of infertility, Team Hagan soared where Kevin and Elizabeth as individuals could not.

Like any new adventure, there would be some bumps as this organization got used to us, especially to me—a liberal pastor with a voice growing stronger every day. But, no matter our anxieties, no matter our uncertainties, no matter what anyone else in our lives thought, we both knew this: God had put this opportunity in the life of our family. On the day Kevin said yes to

Feed the Children, he became the surrogate father of hundreds of thousands of precious children around the world. The enormity of such an awesome responsibility did not register right away.

As we prepared for the transition, it helped that we'd not have to move our lives completely to Oklahoma anytime soon. Kevin still frequently needed to take meetings in Washington, D.C., so the security blanket of my pastoral identity would not be ripped off quite yet. We'd see each other as much as we could—something that would be extremely hard for so many couples, but a challenge we welcomed. Lately we'd grown so much better at talking through our concerns with one another aloud, in person or not.

To gain strength for all that lie ahead, Kevin kept reaching in his pocket, rubbing the black rock with a slight crease down the middle that he'd kept with him every day since my sermon. Each time he felt the small stone, he remembered the invitation and the promise: "Go feed my children. And one day you'll have your own."

The phrase "you'll have your own" bewildered us and simultaneously filled us with hope. Words from God are never like messages found in fortune cookies or decrees from psychic readers.

What did "have our own mean"? Where were said children coming from? When were we going to meet them?

Would we meet some child in a developing country that we'd want to adopt?

Would the fertility doctor have some new brilliant idea that would finally lead to pregnancy for me?

Would something even beyond our wildest dreams show up and change things even more?

We really didn't know. But we believed that God had asked us to dream down this path. Whatever the future held, I sensed that God had given us this word to encourage us. In this calling to Feed the Children, both Kevin and I felt that God had seen us—a comfort that our battle with infertility largely took away. We had so much love to give children.

Just as St. Julian of Norwich had proclaimed centuries before us, "All will be well. All matter of things will be well," Kevin and I slowly began to trust and to hope. Feed the Children was giving us this gift.

We would be parents, somehow; and, in the meantime, we'd help feed some children.

13

Saved by the Sisterhood

Several weeks before Kevin reported for his first day at Feed the Children, I opted to telecommute for a week of work and join him on a business trip in Omaha, Nebraska. I'd never been to Nebraska and saw the week of being with Kevin in a new place as a fun adventure—a welcome distraction from "fertility land." Kevin needed to transition some relationships in the Omaha office of his previous company to his replacement. I needed to work on worship plans for the summer in some peace and quiet. And, if I was really serious about this book project I'd committed to back in Sedona, then I needed time away from the church to write. And, to top it off, our trip fell around Valentine's Day—a time I couldn't *not* be with Kevin.

As we planned the trip, Kevin found us a residence suite complete with a kitchen and sitting room, perfect for the time I'd spend alone during the day. Once we checked into the hotel, I found a cute French bakery nearby that made mouthwatering blueberry muffins. At night we explored the city, slipping and sliding over snowy roads to try new restaurants. The longer we were away, the more breathing space I had to begin thinking about my life more as a writer and less as a full-time pastor. I liked how the rhythm of it felt.

True to normal Hagan fashion, we were rushing to make our flight home from the airport on Friday afternoon. Sitting on the side of the bed with our suitcases packed and standing upright in front of me, I noticed it was already ten minutes past the time that Kevin said he would be back. I called Kevin to figure out what was up. I was even more annoyed when his phone went straight to voicemail. "Oh, he must be on yet another business call," I thought. I hated how many of these he seemed to have at the most inopportune times of the day.

Luckily, before I could get too upset, he barged in the door and said, "I'm sorry I'm late. I'm hurrying. I'm hurrying. I have something to tell you, though. I just got off the phone with the doctor."

"*The* doctor?"

Clinging to the hope of the rock story—that we need not give up on our dream to add children to our family—we had visited the fertility office again weeks earlier to discuss how to proceed after three rounds of IUI failure.

"Well," the doc had said, "There is one test we've never done. Maybe we should do it—just to be 100% sure we know what we are dealing with. We really should have gotten you pregnant by now."

"Well, of course!" Kevin and I exclaimed in union. We thought we'd been through every test imaginable. But if there was one more blood test or exam or whatever, why not?

"We don't usually test your DNA unless there is some extensive history of fertility problems or if the woman is much older than Elizabeth and has had several miscarriages. But if we do this test, we can be 100 percent sure that we know what we are dealing with."

So maybe this was *the* phone call with *the* news.

Kevin rolled his bags toward the door. I stopped him. "Hold up, partner. You've got something to tell me. Is it bad news?"

Being familiar with the bad news/good news drill, he asked, "What do you want to hear first?"

"The bad."

Kevin came over and sat on the bed next to me, leaving his computer bag sitting by the door. *Uh oh... We were sitting down.*

"Well, you know that test they did a couple weeks ago..." Kevin had that look in his eye that said, "I'm about to hurt you, but I really don't want to."

He continued: "Well...it's you."

"It's me? What? What could be wrong with *me*?"

"Well, the doc seemed as shocked as you are because you've been so medically perfect, apart from a cyst now and then."

With a smile I boasted: "I know; they keep saying my uterus is beautiful."

"Well, nothing has changed about that, but something is wrong with your genetic make-up."

"What?? My genetic make-up? How could that be? Am I okay?"

"You're fine. Nothing is wrong with your health. You'll keep living your life like a normal person, but you were born with your thirteenth and fourteenth chromosomes reversed."

"What does that mean??"

"Well, when you were conceived, instead of your chromosomes attaching correctly, they reversed, and part of the thirteenth attached to part of the fourteenth and part of the fourteenth attached to part of the thirteenth, which means that even though you turned out okay…"

"Yes, look at me! I turned out just fine."

"Your ability to reproduce successfully is hindered. People with this condition are 50 percent more likely to miscarry or to birth a child with severe disabilities like Down syndrome. But the good news is that there is a test they can do the next time we do IVF. They can biopsy our embryos on day three of their life, look at their chromosomes, and only put the good ones back in."

"Oh. Wow."

"Are you okay?"

"Give me a minute. But we've got to get to the airport!"

We shut the door of the hotel room. Kevin and rolled both of our bags down the long hallway toward the hotel's elevator. He pushed the button for Floor #1. We faced each other. I spoke first: "I think this is good."

Kevin looked surprised. I imagined minutes before when he told me, he'd been mentally prepared for a full-on Elizabeth Hagan break down.

"How so?"

"Well, I think this news makes me feel less crazy. You know all those times when I thought I was pregnant and then wasn't?"

"Yeah…"

"Well, this sounds like the reason. My body just wanted to naturally abort what it knew it couldn't carry to term. My chromosomes…were the problem all along! And they can do something to fix it!"

We got off the elevator and moved toward the revolving doors. I know Kevin couldn't believe I was taking it so well! I kept telling him over and over what great news we'd received.

I called Marie in the taxi on the way. I knew she'd be just as thrilled. And she was (since I was)!

So, months later, we found ourselves back on the IVF bandwagon with a new plan with treatment #8: (1) make embryos with my eggs plus Kevin's sperm; (2) biopsy the embryos before placing them in me; (3) only put in the ones that were genetically correct. With a 50 percent chance of some of them being identified as good, this seemed like a reasonable move. The doctor knew something new to do that would help make an embryo that would grow into a deliverable baby. Of course, I didn't look forward to the fertility schedule—again involving more early morning tests, more shots, more scheduling uncertainty. But, I was filled with new hope, so I aligned my body in the direction of the routine I knew well. IVF #8, here we come!

When the day of the egg retrieval arrived, I only produced six viable eggs (my lowest count ever). Oh, the tears I cried feeling like such a failure, especially considering that now we knew the odds were that only three of them would make usable embryos. But, what do you do other than keep on keeping on? I hoped some of the embryos would make it through the night. I directed lots of "Sweet baby Jesus's" toward the clinic's lab before we drove home. The next morning the doctor called to say that we had four embryos left. I shouted out in my car on the way to church, "We got four! Four embryos!"

The fertility doc forecast that the day of the transfer would be five days later. We'd just need to decide how many we'd put in—depending, of course, on how many of the embryos had good genes, post genetic biopsy. So, more waiting. More hoping. More living with the terror of the unknown.

I counted my blessings that day five of the embryos' lives fell on a Saturday, not on Pentecost Sunday one day later. What would I have told the church? You'll have to wear red and raise Spirit flags without me because I'm getting impregnated?

Saturday morning, I woke up around 7:00 a.m., unusually early for not-a-morning-person me. I left Kevin alone and moved toward our adjoining walk-in closet where I kept long-sleeve t-shirts—perfect to throw on during nippy mornings like this. I put on my softest one from a church camp I had once chaperoned. Then, my feet wanted socks. I found my favorite slippers, with pumpkins on them—the ones Kevin had given me when we first started this whole IVF mess a couple years ago now. I put them on for luck. I planned to go downstairs, pour myself a glass of orange juice, and make some oatmeal. I'd take my phone with me, so to not wake Kevin. I'd breathe in, breathe out, and prepare mentally for this day to come.

But before I got past even our bedroom door, my phone rang. *No way! This early?*

Like a hot potato, I threw the phone on top of the bed in the direction of Kevin. He startled awake at the noise, but buried deeper still under our fluffy grey comforter.

"I think it's her. I think it's her. You talk to her!"

And it was.

Perking up quickly, he said in a scratchy, I-haven't-talked-to-anyone-yet-this-morning voice: "Hello, this is Kevin." He used the same tone answering his business calls from work.

And, immediately, I ran. I ran downstairs out of earshot of the phone and curled up in a ball on the living room couch under a fuzzy blanket. I didn't want to know the news until I had to.

Kevin slowly emerged from the staircase minutes later. His steps sounded tempered and intentional. So it was bad news. I knew it. I uncurled from the fetal position and looked up at him.

And Kevin said: "The chromosomes looked horrible."

"They did? All of them?"

"Yes, all of them. She said if we did the transfer today there is no way that we'd get pregnant. She read me the numbers but all I heard was they're abnormal beyond abnormal. It's over."

I gasped. Kevin went on, "She threw me back to 'every cycle is different.' We can keep trying if we want…"

We met in the middle of the couch, embracing as deep wells of sadness re-emerged from our ducts. We cried and cried in one another's arms.

But, after several minutes, I was done. I just couldn't cry anymore. I couldn't be held anymore. I told Kevin I didn't want to mope around like we'd done with similar phone calls. I wanted to move on and move on right then.

I started making a list of house projects we needed to work on right away. You know, all of those life tasks everybody eventually needs to get to but rarely makes time for? We'd do them. All of them. Kevin fell in line. So off to the bank to open up that safety deposit box we'd always said we'd get, then to the grocery store to buy a month's worth of toilet paper and paper towels (since I found several coupons in a sale flyer soon to expire), then to the home organization store to find a container to hold extra plastic bags—I was so tired of them being strewn across the kitchen! I allowed us one break at 10:00 a.m. for breakfast, but only if we didn't dawdle.

As we stuffed our mouths with blueberry pancakes at a diner blocks from our house, I knew it was over. Being still long enough in the booth meant I couldn't avoid the truth. We would not try again. My eggs seemed worse than we even imagined. There was no reason to continue this heartbreak!

From booth #10, I said aloud these words I *never, ever,* wanted to be true: "I will not have biological children."

Syrup ran from my fork to my puffy vest. I choked back some orange juice. Pancake crumbs dribbled down the side of my mouth. I knew I would never feel the miracle of a child growing in my belly. I would never ask Kevin to take me to the hospital because my water had broken. I would never post one of those after-birth photos with a new mother glow, causing commentators to swoon. I would not experience some of the amazing parts of what it means be a woman that I'd long hoped for. Ever.

I told Kevin to pay the bill quickly and suggested we abandon our list. He agreed and proposed a marathon of the worst reality shows for the rest of the day. Let's laugh at something ridiculous, we both thought.

We did not leave the couch for hours. And, by nightfall, I was throwing all of my energy into editing Sunday's sermon. I wasn't quite sure it had a point, but at least it was an effort. If the church people only knew the mindset of the preacher behind their sermon, they'd either appreciate me tenfold or think I'd lost my mind and send me home. I didn't give them the chance to make that call.

In less than 24 hours, Pastor Elizabeth was in full action. I taught Sunday school. I consulted with Andy, our music minister, about the special music for the day. I climbed into the pulpit when it was my time to do so on Pentecost Sunday wearing red high heels and a plastered smile. I proclaimed the wonders of the Spirit of God, who never left us orphaned. It was one sermon of which I didn't believe a word when I preached it. I felt like shit, but loved my congregation enough to try to give them what they needed.

By Tuesday afternoon, in the quietness of the pastor's study, I began to write a Taylor Swift-like "We are never, ever, ever getting back together" email to our fertility doctor. I came to the last sentence and prepared to hit send when my inbox chimed with a new message. I saved my break-up note in the draft folder and I checked the inbox to see what had arrived.

Marie's name filled the "from" memo line. I started reading right away:

From one sister to another, I've been having a thought float around in my head and guess I might as well get it off my chest… If you decide to do another round of IVF again, I'd be willing to go through the process with you. Perhaps they could harvest my eggs along with yours and then you would have even more potential? We could be on crazy drugs together at the same time… Wouldn't that be a hoot? I'm not even sure what the chances of donor eggs taking are? How close a match to DNA we have to have, if any, etc. I won't mention it again, but if you ever want to talk about it just let me know, I'd be glad to give you some of mine.

    Love,
    Marie

Oh, my God. Oh, my God. I fell to the floor and wept. And wept and wept full of glee.

What Marie did not know was that I'd stayed up late the previous night in bed dissecting our situation rationally just one more time. In the wee hours of the morning, I played a game of "what we knew" and "what we needed to make a baby." I couldn't fully let the dream of biological children go until I was completely sure it was 100 percent over.

To make a baby we first needed sperm. We knew Kevin had less than optimal sperm, but it could be "fixed" in the lab. Our doc's lab proved our sperm could be fertilized well.

Second, we needed eggs. We knew my eggs sucked. Obviously, a huge problem.

Third, we needed a good womb to carry the child. We knew I had a good womb. My uterus was routinely called "gorgeous" during ultrasounds, after all.

So if we wanted a baby and didn't want to be thrown back into the potential adoption hell we had already been through once…we needed eggs.

We needed eggs that made babies.

From 1:00 to 2:00 a.m. that night, I thought about how I felt about this.

Contrary to Kevin's thought process with the idea of sperm donation, I did not want to buy eggs from some anonymous donor. I knew the going rate for donated eggs was up to $10,000. My thrifty self thought it both outrageous and too much like baby-buying (though for those who felt comfortable doing this, I completely understood). So around 2:30 a.m., this is where I landed: If I couldn't have a child biologically, I'd want its genetic make-up to come from someone I loved, who gave the gift to us out of love and a desire to be in our lives forever as an *extra-special* family member.

Staring up at the dark ceiling, I went through a list of whose eggs I would consider (*not that they were offering, but just in case*).

Meredith was out. She'd needed a hysterectomy after the birth of her last child. Her eggs were gone.

Lucy was out. She'd not yet had kids of her own. It would not be appropriate to take from her even if she offered.

But then there was Marie. Marie already had her daughter. Marie and I had always lovingly called each other sisters. I loved Marie's family like my own. Marie and Bob had already offered us Bob's sperm. They understood how much we wanted a family. Marie was a perfect choice and really the only choice. No one else's name made my list.

Yet, simultaneously, I knew I'd never ask Marie. It's not like I could ever start a conversation like, "Hey, Marie, can you give me some of your eggs?" Even for me, and even with how open I'd become throughout this process, such a request was too taboo.

But just for fun, I brought the idea up with Kevin while we sat side by side on the couch watching the news the following morning. He wanted to know what had kept me up so late tossing and turning. I explained my whole thought process.

"Well, I hear you. You and Marie are such good friends. But I agree with you, you could never ask!"

Now here I was at 4:00 p.m. on the same day, only hours after I'd mused about this very thing, reading Marie's email. How could I not believe in God at a moment like this? Maybe this was God's strange but wonderful way of sending us children. Not only would my future child have life, but also I'd be receiving the life-giving gift of deep community in the process! Wasn't this what abundant living looked like?

My weeping in the fetal position on the rug in front of my study desk lasted for at least an hour. Overwhelmed with Marie's gift, overwhelmed with hope-filled resurrection possibilities, overwhelmed with God's sense of timing and love for us, I could do nothing else. If I'd had any appropriate CDs in my office, I might have started singing and soul clapping too. I didn't care who might have heard me in the church this time. If someone had stopped by and asked what was going on with my wailing for joy, I'm sure I would have told them. The news felt just that good.

Luckily, my 5:00 p.m. pre-marital counseling appointment canceled. I could go home earlier than expected. When I dialed Kevin on the drive, he sensed my glee-filled excitement right away. And the wonder of it all is that he said, "Let's go for it if she's serious. I'm okay too." How in the world did Kevin and I go from the death of a dream to a gift of life in a matter of hours?

From my living room, I called Marie as I stood staring out the blinds of my front door. My first words to Marie came in awe. "I love you beyond my ability to say, Marie."

"I love you too, Elizabeth."

"Sisters forever, right?"

"Sisters forever."

Both being planners, we moved on to the details before either of us got off the phone. I told her I didn't want my eggs involved anymore. I wanted hers, just hers. More tears flowed down my face. I could hear her sniffling too.

I added: "I want to be as open about this process as we can. I would feel no shame in telling the world what you are doing for us…and our baby!"

Marie volunteered to start weaning her six-month-old daughter as soon as possible to prepare for the upcoming procedure. (She'd already started reading up on what it required.) She promised to have a consultation with her doctor about his thoughts on the idea. I promised to get an appointment with our fertility doctor ASAP to share our new and exciting plan!

My can-do disposition again went into overdrive. Within days, both our doctors proved supportive and committed to working together, though in different states. Kevin and I scheduled an appointment with the lawyer with whom we'd first talked about adoption, arranging to complete the necessary legal paperwork.

Our doctors proposed that Marie go through all the pre-IVF tests that I'd been through numerous times, but in her hometown clinic. Then, when it was close to time for Marie's eggs to come out, she would travel to D.C. so that the fertilization could take place in my clinic, with her eggs and Kevin's sperm. The embryos would go in my uterus afterward.

The beginnings of our #9 IVF started to take shape. Marie didn't know what to expect, but seemed open to whatever came. As the drug regimen began, it was strangely gratifying to me to become her "IVF coach," sharing how I'd learned to cope. This intensely lonely process did not feel so isolating anymore. Yet, I felt horrible about the side affects Marie experienced. Large doses of estrogen meant intense mood swings and cramps; but when I apologized, Marie would brush it off like no big deal. She kept repeating, "I want to do this for you."

But then, one afternoon over the phone, she confessed, "I think of you, Elizabeth, all the time now. Every time I exercise, every time I make a good food choice, and every time I say no to alcohol, just as I would do if I were trying to get pregnant myself, I think of you."

"You do?" I asked incredulously.

"Yes! I want do everything I can to make a strong and healthy baby for you!"

Who gets an amazing best friend like this? Apparently, I did.

I loved her with the deep love I now knew possible to experience in this world, and this greatest gift of a friend loved me the same. I know that Marie feared the procedure not working and the subsequent disappointment we'd both share, but I kept telling her, "You just don't understand. Of course, I hope it works, but how could I ever be mad at you? This is the most amazing outpouring of love I've ever known. When I think about our future, no matter what happens, all I can think of is love."

It seemed that trusting in the divine mystery of things was way better than I ever could have planned. Marie and I were making a baby.

14

Into Africa

Proving that the Hagans never take the simply option in life, in the midst of our IVF cycle with Marie, the idea of an Africa trip emerged. The staff of Feed the Children in Malawi and Kenya invited Kevin to visit. The goals of the trip would include seeing the feeding, education, and health programs in these countries and meeting members of his international staff. The sooner he traveled there, the better. To lead well he needed to know who he was leading. And, though Kevin possessed an international affairs master's degree, he'd never set foot in Africa.

Kevin wanted to know if I would go too. Of course! I'd traveled extensively on service trips in Africa before I met him, and since then it had been a goal of mine to do a trip like this together. I couldn't wait to see Kevin in an environment without regular hot running water. I knew he'd freak out when the power went out for no reason. I knew he'd hate how much he'd have to use hand sanitizer. I knew he'd squirm a little when he was stuck in a sweaty van on bumpy roads for hours on end. I both wanted to make fun of his discomfort and to help him along the way. I knew that without a buddy in such an unfamiliar environment, he might not come across as the shining star of leadership that he was! And, though some friends who knew about our fertility plans wondered why I didn't stay home, my doctor said I could go—with the condition that I'd take my hormone pills every day. Taking pills was something I could do anywhere. So why not go?

And so, with open hearts, our long journey across the pond began. Two long flights and twenty hours later, we laid eyes on Lilongwe, Malawi. As our feet hit the hot pavement, our eyes hung heavy with jet lag, and our jelly-filled legs barely managed to place one wobbly foot in front of the other. We pulled off our jackets, feeling the hot sun on our backs, and reached for our sunglasses in our backpacks. The stench of body odor mixed with the thickness of the humidity assaulted us. Other Euro-Americans and Europeans on our flight looked disoriented from the start. Wiping sweat from their foreheads, they wore the startled expressions of those who'd landed in no man's land. However, for me the sea of black and brown faces, the bright clothes, and fellow passengers speaking Swahili felt familiar and welcoming. We cleared customs quickly. Then, the hundred-plus of us who had just disembarked stood shoulder to shoulder in a crowded room. Several flies swarmed around my head. I daydreamed about how great it would be to have cool water on my lips again, for I was more than thirsty. But, instead, we focused on finding Kevin's large black suitcase and my pink one. I glanced at Kevin. Africa rookie or not, I could tell he was ready for the adventure.

We found Feed the Children's country director right away, the white man holding a sign with our names on it. He offered us water bottles and delivered us to one of Lilongwe's hotels for a couple hours of rest. The hotel, similar at first glance to a Motel 6 in America, was clean. However, it didn't have running water or power.

"What am I gonna do? What I am I gonna do?" Kevin exclaimed as he began to unpack his suitcase. "I can't go to dinner with my suit looking like this! And no shower... How am I going to greet people tonight without bathing?" (*We later learned the hotel conserved power every afternoon from 3–6 p.m. as part of the normal routine.*)

I calmed Kevin down, reminding him wrinkles in your clothes are okay and suggesting maybe we didn't smell that bad. We'd just have to roll with it. After a while, he started listening and thanked me repeatedly: "I'm so glad you are here." (*It would be another ten hours before we got our first shower.*)

On the third and last day of our time in Malawi, with so much joy in our hearts from all the children we'd seen smile because of the aid of Feed the Children, Kevin and the other staffers cloistered themselves in the country's office to finish up some administrative tasks. No need for me to stick around. Not wanting me to be bored, the staff wondered if I would like to visit an orphanage that Feed the Children supplied with food. It was staffed by the Sisters of Charity (the order of Mother Teresa). I, of course, said I would love to visit. Mother Teresa was one of my spiritual heroes. The idea of being so close to some of her sisters felt like an opportunity I couldn't pass up. But, I overlooked the one key word in the invitation: *orphanage*.

In the car I got the shakes. As we approached the orphanage gate, my driver asked: "Are you okay, Miss?" I guess he saw fear in my eyes that I didn't want to admit was there. I was about to visit a real-life orphanage, a home for children who did not have parents.

Slowly, I walked toward the gated entrance and then the first room: the baby room. The smell of twenty-plus children, not bathed regularly and in need of diaper changes, rushed at me like a mighty wind. Two young Malawian women, probably not a day over twenty years old, served as the room's caregivers. No Catholic sisters in sight.

As I surveyed the scene, memories of watching documentaries about the conditions of Romanian children in orphanages flashed through my head. It had always seemed surreal on the screen, but, before my eyes, it was real—this room stuffed with cribs. I could not move from one end to the other without bumping into rails. Some of the babies crawled around this maze of confusion. Others jumped up and down in their cribs like prisoners ready to break out at any moment. Others lay prostrate crying. One caregiver just sat on one side of the room, apparently annoyed by all the noise. The other woman changed the diaper of a baby boy while three others grabbed her legs, asking for attention.

My natural instinct was to pick a baby up. But (*one huge but*), I'd long ago given up holding little ones. Babies broke my heart. Babies reminded me of my pain. I stayed as far away from the church nursery every Sunday as possible. As much as I wanted to grow the church with young families, I was so glad our church nursery hosted only one baby on most Sundays, and other times none at all. But, with these babies before me, I could not be cruel. I needed to touch one. They needed me. My eyes were soon drawn to a happy little girl in a crib, no more than nine months old, who was reaching out her hands in my direction. She had the biggest brown sparkling eyes.

Before I had time to second-guess my decision, I moved in her direction. Hoisting her up, I wrapped her legs around my waist and I looked into her brown eyes. I laid her sweet face on my shoulder. And with this skin-to-skin touch on my collarbone, tears began to stream down my face. We nestled in together. The baby pulled at my hair with her little hands. She grabbed for my earrings. But, surprisingly, I didn't flinch. I was so happy to have her in my arms.

Beside me stood my driver, a baby on his hip as well. He spoke great English. I wanted to know more. "Why are most of these kids here? Do they have any chance of adoption?"

"Most likely their mothers died from AIDS or they're sick and no family members want to take care of them. They'll be in an institution for life. Few Malawian families have the funds to take in another child."

Wow! All of this, on top of the fact that I learned earlier in the day that Americans are not allowed to adopt in Malawi (*well, unless you are Madonna and give the government millions of dollars*). Deep, deep sigh. *Don't lose it, Elizabeth—not in public. Please don't lose it now.*

I bounced the baby girl up and down on my hip, hoping to get her to laugh. She soon smiled. I smiled back.

Oh, but I wanted to weep for hours! My heart sank when I thought of both of our futures, hers as an orphan who probably would never be adopted, and mine as childless mother who cannot be hers. I have so much to give, but she can't receive it.

As the driver motioned to me, saying, "Let's move," I put my bright-eyed girl back in her crib as slowly as I could. I whispered a prayer for this little one's future, rubbing sleep out of her eyes and saying: "God loves you, sweet little friend. And I do too."

After seeing more of the same in other rooms, I kept my distance. I would not pick up another Malawian child. *Not another Malawian child.*

I buried my head in the pillow for hours when the driver dropped me off back at the hotel. I told Kevin, "Don't ever leave me alone on this trip again!"

Soon we boarded a plane, headed to Kenya by way of a stopover in Zambia. I'd last been to Kenya as an eighteen-year-old, leading summer camp for missionary kids. Though eager to see this beautiful country again, I still felt shaken by the orphanage in Malawi. I didn't know how much more sadness I could take in! Upon arrival, our crew faced the horrors of traffic in Nairobi, creeping along at a snail's pace. Kevin and I sat in the sedan of the regional director, Shiphrah, who'd just met us at the airport.

Shiphrah, a European woman, told us right away of her a long history in Kenya. She'd been in Africa for many years already with Feed the Children. She seemed personable, asking me lots of questions about our time in Malawi, but I gave one or two word answers. I rarely looked her direction. With the pain I was still processing from the previous days, I didn't have much energy for this friendly woman sitting beside me.

On the side of the city nearest to our lodging, our group shared a quick dinner of samosas, chicken, and vegetables. After Shiphrah and her driver dropped us off at the guesthouse where we'd stay for the duration of our trip, Kevin noticed my pacing around our little room and asked, "What's wrong?" It was bedtime.

I told him I wasn't excited about the plan of visiting the Feed the Children home the next day, a place also filled with children who were without parents. This children's center in Nairobi was one of two that Feed the Children owned and operated internationally. Our orientation packet told us that many of the kids there lived with special needs. We'd spend the entire day tomorrow with the children and staff.

In the weeks leading up to our departure to Africa, Shiphrah, having learned I was a pastor, had asked me give a devotion at the beginning of the opening meeting. Normally, I would have been thrilled! Being invited to speak at a special event equaled a great honor in my book. Yet after what I'd seen in Malawi, I no longer thought I could stomach being in a community of orphans, much less giving a sermon to them. What could I possibly say without sobbing?

As we laid our heads on the pillow and lowered the mosquito nets around our bed, I pushed Kevin: "Couldn't you just leave me here tomorrow, saying I was sick?"

He reminded me how bad it would look if I came all this way as an ambassador for this organization and then bailed. I had come on this trip to support him, not the other way around. *Who knew so soon it would be his turn to carry me?*

Kevin promised, "I'll be with you, my love. Don't worry. If it gets to be too much, you can just squeeze my hand and we'll make up a reason to leave the room." Well, okay. At least we'd established a back-up plan.

In the morning, I slid on navy cargo pants, a loose-fitting pink cotton blouse, and tennis shoes. With no time to dry my hair, I put some mousse in it, hoping I'd look enough like the wife of the president to pass the eye test. I willed a couple of bites of egg into my mouth at the breakfast table in the building next to our house. Then, I strapped on our blue backpack—carrying all of Kevin's notebooks and materials for the day and emergency snacks—before climbing into the van sent to pick up us and our four other traveling companions. I held Kevin's hand tightly in the car, mouthing to him at least twice: "Back-up plan—remember!" Yet before I felt ready to face the day, our van was already pulling onto the property.

"Well, hello," Shiphrah said as she opened the car door for us. Kevin crawled out first, and I followed.

"How did you rest last night?"

I noticed right away the power in Shiphrah's stride and the compassion in her hands. Shiphrah was short and slim, barely over five feet tall, with short brown hair. She wore crisply ironed navy pants with a bright red top under a fitted white jacket with a silver pendant on the lapel. With trendy white leather tennis shoes that looked freshly polished, her put-together exterior matched her inner confidence. How had I not had eyes to see her joy in the car ride the night before?

Kevin spoke up: "Well, fine. We slept fine."

(If he was talking about me, who'd tossed and turned well into the midnight hour, he'd just lied).

"Great! Come on inside. We have some visitors who want to meet you."

After being escorted to a yellow couch that sat parallel to Shiphrah's desk, some children appeared at the door, four of them in all, each dressed in what I would call their "Sunday best" with white sashes stretching diagonally across their chests. As the kids came closer, three walking and one in a wheelchair, I noticed the word *usher* and then their name sown into each of their sashes.

These kids seemed nothing like the children I'd encountered days before in Malawi. They smiled. They wore pressed clothes. They had clean faces. They helped us feel so welcome.

My mind drifted to dreading the sight of more babies in my future, but Shiphrah was on task and spoke directly to me in her British accent: "What hymn do you want sung before your sermon, Elizabeth?"

"Um. My sermon? I thought I'd be just giving a devotion? I've only got ten minutes or so prepared."

I shouldn't have been surprised. I'd been warned by ordained colleagues that, on trips like this, a sermon—and a long one at that—could be asked of me at any time.

"Oh, it doesn't matter. I'm sure whatever you have to say will be fine. What shall we sing?"

After flipping through the paperback hymnal she handed me, I came up with "Count Your Many Blessings," a hymn we'd always sung at family Thanksgivings growing up. Shiphrah said,

"Good choice. It's a hymn they love to sing." A good sign, I thought; at least I'd made one right decision. My "loose" plan was to speak about staying strong through discouraging life experiences, drawing from 2 Corinthians 4:1–12. A piece of paper in my Bible contained some scribbled notes, but without my normal eight-page, fourteen-point font, single-spaced, marked-up preaching manuscript, I felt a bit unprepared. *Oh, well.*

Our ushers for the day escorted Kevin and me to the main dining hall for the opening program. We took our places in the front row in the chairs with signs that read, "President" and "First Lady." I second-guessed my outfit choice for the day as I looked out at the over three hundred staff and children seated behind and beside us, all dressed in bright primary colors—a sea of bright red, green, and yellow polo shirts. The pride with which the workers carried themselves showed they had put on their best to meet their new president and his wife. *Was that really us?*

The service began as we sang "Count Your Many Blessings" with gusto. I could hardly mouth the fourth verse because my tears were flowing so copiously. Music always moves my soul in ways deeper than I could express with words, and going to church in Kenya, it seemed, multiplied the movement. Next came the children's choir that offered a special musical piece with drums, followed by a staff choir leading us in "Great Is Thy Faithfulness." Kevin passed me tissues from his pants pocket because I could not hold back the flow. I didn't want to be known as the First Lady of Snot.

Next came prayers of installation for Kevin and a "litany of recommitment" by the staff to serve under Kevin's leadership. The pastor in me couldn't have been more impressed with the thoughtfulness of the service planning, or more in awe of the feeling of God's presence. It was the first time since that day at church with the rocks that both Kevin and I felt affirmed in the spiritual calling of our huge leap into Feed the Children. And in all of this, slowly the dreaded anticipation of seeing babies left my memory. I abided in the moment for the first time in many hours and couldn't wait to proclaim the goodness of God at the end of the program, when it was my time!

When the emcee handed me the microphone, I voiced a quick prayer for the congregation, but did so with eyes open, looking each child and staffer in the eyes (*different from my normal practice*). On this very special day, I wanted to see them. I wanted them to know I already loved them. I wanted to share something of value from scripture with them. I opened my Bible with the largest grin I could muster, charging forth with the confidence of knowing I had a word to offer. It came some from my notes, but more from how the service in the past few minutes had moved me. I knew for sure that God was with us in this new journey together. I spoke of this. Kevin later told me, "I'm so proud of you! Wow!"

Afterward, as we took a tour of the large campus, Shiphrah walked alongside of me. "I hear you are a writer as well as a pastor?" I was impressed! No one on the trip had picked up on this important part of my identity. "I read your blog a couple of days ago," she shared. And, with that, Shiphrah and I dived into a conversation about the spiritual meaning of dreams I'd just written about. I was in heaven.

The next morning, Shiphrah came to pick us up with her driver. The agenda for Sunday morning, our off day, included a visit to an elephant orphanage. We'd watch a feeding of the baby elephants rescued in the wild. Then, we'd go to lunch. The other staffers in our group planned to join us later. Kevin and I both felt excited about seeing wildlife.

When our car arrived at the elephant orphanage, Shiphrah, Kevin, and I sat in our vehicle, debriefing the previous day's events. Kevin complimented Shiphrah on what amazing work he could tell she was doing with the kids. We both told her how much we'd loved the previous day's program, the beauty of the grounds of the children's center, and how proud we were to support this organization alongside of her.

As we kept talking, Kevin told Shiphrah more about our lives prior to Feed the Children. Somehow the conversation quickly got very personal. I couldn't believe what I heard. Kevin told her why we didn't have children, how frustrating our fertility journey had become, and even that we had tried adoption only to be met with more failure. I feared Kevin's openness. Was he really going there? Uttering the word *adoption* was not just a conversational pleasantry; it sat at the heart of our story in a way no one at Feed the Children knew about. And we had only just met Shiphrah! How could he possibly trust her so soon?

Yet, the longer the three of us sat in the car together, the more something about Shiphrah made us both feel as if we could talk to her as much as we needed. She listened with her eyes, reflecting back love and concern. I eventually joined in too. Taking turns detailing the story, we used the words *weeping, disappointment,* and *failure* over and over again. And, with tears welling up, I told Shiphrah all about Malawi and about those crying babies gripping my legs. Shiphrah reached into her purse and found some tissues, resting her hand my knee. As I blew my nose, Kevin spoke of the center again, this time highlighting how he couldn't get those kids out of his mind. He really wanted to adopt. Of course, I thought the kids were cute, and I would love to take any of them home with us (*isn't that what most people say coming home from a humanitarian trip?*), but...

Shiphrah piped in, "Don't say you can't adopt. *You can.* We've seen European families adopt kids from our center all the time. Why not an American family like you both? You just have to commit to live in Kenya for six to nine months to complete the process."

I piped in right away to object: "I can't move to Kenya for that long! I have a job. I have a life back home."

What direct and unafraid people the three of us were in our sedan sanctuary! Shiphrah looked me in the eyes and said, "You can, Elizabeth. You can. You've said you're a writer, right?" I nodded. "You could move here and live near us. You could write your book in my garden." She paused, and then went on, "You know I used to be a midwife, don't you?" It was true, I remembered reading this in her bio that Kevin received before the trip. "Well, you could do this, and I could be your spiritual midwife, helping you through the process."

Though Shiphrah knew nothing of my own birthing story yet, and only some of the pain, I couldn't believe her offer. Shiphrah's offer came directly from her heart and landed in mine. She straightaway volunteers to be my spiritual midwife? She volunteers to be in the trenches of the spiritual and emotional delivery room with me? She wants to help me birth something? Who *was* this woman? My heart leapt a thousand beats a second, pounding out the rhythm of a "Yes!" Maybe Kenyan adoption was for us?

Soon, the time came to get out of our little car and head toward the elephants. Kevin and I walked side-by-side, forming a line with Shiphrah as if we we'd long ago choreographed our togetherness. Shiphrah slipped me more Kleenex and a hat as we approached the viewing mound and said, "Wear my hat, my dear. You don't want to get burnt at this high of an elevation." Thankfully, it was an appropriate occasion to wear sunglasses—for, oh, the story my eyes could have told at that very moment that I wasn't yet ready to tell.

By time we got back to our guesthouse for the night, Kevin and I finally had some alone time to talk. We both felt overwhelmed by what had happened to us in the car, struck by the directness of Shiphrah's words and how those words had resonated in our spirits. And, as I hung close to Shiphrah over the next couple of days, the unexpected continued.

When we visited a maternity clinic deep in the bush two hours from the Nairobi city center, Shiphrah made me promise her I'd assist her with a delivery if time came for a mother to give birth. I said yes. *What?!?*

When we spent five hours together in the car on the way to a school feeding on the other side of the country, I told Shiphrah more details about the deep layers of grief the years of infertility had loaded on my shoulders—something I'd never done with someone I'd just met.

When, one day, our schedule took us back to the children's center, Shiphrah said she and I had work to do—without Kevin or anyone else. Shiphrah took me into the baby cottage. I was afraid, of course, but I agreed. We took our shoes off in cottage one, the newborn-to-age-one room. Over fifteen babies filled the space, with content looks on their faces. Some slept in cribs in the adjoining room. Some lay on the floor holding stuffed animals. Most of the rest were held by house moms feeding, changing, or burping them—a night and day difference from Malawi!

I found my way to a rocking chair, hoping to just observe and keep my distance. But Shiphrah, of course, would have none of it! Soon she placed in my arms a newborn baby girl wearing a pink onesie with purple daisies all over. Baby girl looked about six months old, already with enough hair to require pulling it back with a barrette. "What's her name?" I asked.

"Faith," they said. "Her name is Faith." As I held Faith, I thought of her future with Feed the Children as her new home: a place where all her needs were met. She'd have a good chance of either being reunited with some relatives or adopted—while, in the meantime, being loved on by some sweet, sweet Feed the Children mamas. When the time came, I could easily give her back to a smiling adult. It was so much easier to do than in Malawi.

And when we reunited with Kevin, I exclaimed, "I held a baby, Kevin, a real live baby." What a good journey it was!

One night before our week in Kenya came to an end, Shiphrah gave us that "Let's take a walk" look before our supper arrived at the restaurant's table. She pointed us to the gardens outside where we could catch up privately.

"So, what are you thinking these days, Hagans?" she asked.

Kevin spoke first. We couldn't stop thinking about the possibilities of adoption. I chimed in: "The more I think about it, Shiphrah, a Kenyan adventure is not out of the picture for what I could envision next in my life."

We could barely see one another's faces, as it was nightfall by now, but we kept talking. Shiphrah said she'd usually not be so forward with her new boss and his wife, but with us the nudge of God to bring up adoption felt so strong.

By the end of the chat, we agreed. Kevin and I said in unison we felt drawn toward Kenyan adoption. We couldn't deny something was at work in our hearts. Our IVF plans with Marie back at home felt as far away as we were from America.

Shiphrah hugged both of us with glee, and said to me, "Elizabeth, congratulations, you are pregnant."

Shiphrah said I was pregnant.

All of three of us hugged each other in silent glee. I broke the silence by saying how sorry I was for being so weepy all week. "Oh, do not apologize. Your water is just beginning to leak with anticipation of all that is to come. I told you you were pregnant, didn't I?"

I beamed back at her, the spiritual dance between us continuing. But what Shiphrah did not know is that I was taking hormone pills every day on the trip with hopes of starting IVF when I returned. So many of my tears came from the extra dose of estrogen I was taking every morning. How the new dream of Kenyan adoption and the old dream of IVF back at home would fit together (or not), I had no idea. But how could I *not* say yes to what my heart leaped toward in this week? We needed more time at home to sort it out, and could tell Shiphrah about it then.

But, as far as the adoption was concerned, Shiphrah, Kevin, and I made a plan: the next day we would stop by the adoption agency in Nairobi, one of the two in the country that assisted couples from the U.S. We'd learn more there and just see what came next. Putting our heads on the pillow that night, Kevin and I felt elated.

At 10:00 a.m. the next day, with cups of good Kenyan tea in our hands, our informational meeting at the agency felt like a big step—but the right one. We appreciated both the encouragement and the honesty of the adoption officers. This would be no easy process, but neither would it be impossible. Climbing back into the car, Shiphrah asked me what I thought. "Well, I assume that couples go into a meeting like that with all of that information thrown at you and then one of two things happens. Either you feel tired already and decide it isn't for you, or you become more resolved than before—like, 'What's a bunch of paperwork? I can do that.'"

I went on after a few moments of silence: "Really, people, what's a bunch of paperwork?"

We laughed together, giving each other the look of knowing we'd just started something really holy.

Lunch of sandwiches and a shared salad at an outdoor café served as the venue for our celebration. What ground we'd covered together over the course of just one week! We toasted our bottles of water in thanksgiving that Operation Kevin and Elizabeth Adopt in Kenya was underway. As Shiphrah hugged us goodbye on the curb of the Nairobi airport, I told her I loved her and we'd keep in touch. We exchanged Skype names. Kevin added: "You should be honored. Elizabeth doesn't normally open up to people as fast as she did to you."

Who would have ever known that Kenya, sweet Kenya, would be the place where resurrection's hope again rekindled my soul? Sure, we'd have to go home and start making big decisions, but, while leaving Kenya that afternoon, I couldn't help but feel overwhelmed with delight.

I hummed one of my favorite hymns all the way home: "Morning by morning, new mercies I see… All I have needed thy hand hath provided…" If a week as surprising as this could breathe new life into us, then all would be well, all matter of things would be well. And, what a gift to have Shiphrah as a friend now!

Leaving the last whiff of African air behind, we boarded a plane headed first to Rome, and, then, twenty hours later, Washington, D.C. We were tired, but preaching my first sermon back at the church several days later, I stood in the pulpit with grounded joy.

We came home from Kenya telling everyone we knew about our adoption plans. Most were thrilled for us. They knew by the delight on our faces that this was not some joke. We made all of our beloveds sit through rounds and rounds of our photos. Really, something special had happened to us. As crazy as it sounded, our African trip gave us a new calling besides Kevin's day-to-day work with Feed the Children. I started working on our home study immediately. We were well on our way.

I dreaded telling Marie, but knew I must soon. When I found the courage to call her, much to my surprise, she voiced her support. Marie and Bob even offered to be the legal guardians of our Kenyan child in case something happened to us (a role our paperwork required). I smiled the rest of the day.

When I told our fertility doctor about the new developments, she offered a solution to our mid-process change of course.

"Why don't you finish the process, but just freeze the embryos?"

"Freeze them?"

"Yeah, that way whenever you're ready, when you want to have a child after you get your other one home, you'll be ready."

Bingo. Truly, we could have it all! In all honestly, I wanted both. Why could I not have both? A biological(ish) child and an adopted one too. And, maybe this was the abundance of God—the "Go feed my children and you'll have your own" promise coming true! I'd arrived at the point where I did not care where my children came from—I just wanted them. And I was so tired of the pain that it took to have them.

For weeks after arriving home, I began church services with this call and response: "God is good. And, all the time, God is good." Church members' eyes reflected back to me, "What's gotten into you, Pastor Elizabeth?"

Around our house, I daydreamed about how we'd organize the nursery/ toddler's room/ big kid's room (for our application forms to the agency said we were open to a child of any age). I thought about how we would integrate Kenyan food and celebration of Kenyan holidays into our family's rhythms. And, when Barack Obama was up for re-election in the fall of 2012, I told Kevin that we'd better vote for him. Would he really want to confess to his future child that he hadn't voted for the first Kenyan-American president?

Fall turned into winter. On the first Sunday of Advent, I shared the hard news with my congregation. In January, I'd leave my position at the church to be ready for the next adventure. I'd devote more time to writing, supporting Kevin's work at Feed the Children, and most of all, becoming ready to be the mama of a Kenyan child. I voiced for the first time the word "infertility" from the pulpit. These were all great leaps of faith into the unknown, but with the support of nurturing voices such as Jean and now Shiphrah, I felt ready to soar!

Finding Our Way

Just as planned, in January I made the 1,500+ mile trek with Kevin to our temporary apartment in Oklahoma City. We filled our car with some of our favorite decorations, half of our wardrobes, and lots of my complaints that we were actually moving to middle America. I would take up residence in a "foreign" land. I *wanted* to learn to like it. Or at least try.

Once we arrived, I kept my chin up, thinking I'd be packing my bags soon for Kenya. So, perhaps this time in Oklahoma was really more like a personal vacation? Or a cultural experiment? Or even the sabbatical I did not stay at my former church long enough to get? I chose to frame my days by calling them the latter, embracing a life of catching up on novels, going to the gym every day, and cooking good meals every night. I baked—*a lot*. Embarking on a seemingly impossible project from our tiny kitchen, I successfully made over 250 heart-shaped cookies-on-a-stick for the Feed the Children staff Valentine's Party. I visited a couple of friends for long weekends, a gift from the lack of Sunday sermons in my schedule. My life felt on hold in many ways—but for a good cause, I told myself.

But then it was May, and then June, with no word on when the Kenyan adoption board would hear our case. Without the liturgical rhythm that had held my grief in check for all these years, I felt lazy, unmotivated, and anxious. I imagined my pastor friends would keep me busy with supply preaching gigs, but between January and May I was only asked to preach twice.

I started to tell Kevin: "I feel trapped." As much as I wanted to adopt, I wanted to work and feel useful again. I also worried that if we settled in Oklahoma permanently, as it was looking as if we would, I'd never be allowed to preach, given that every time I opened my mouth to say, "I'm a pastor," in this new city, folks looked at me as if I had ten heads. My unemployed spirit drooped in despair. My days of exclaiming, "God is good, all the time!" from the pulpit in Virginia felt like four years ago, not four months!

I kept praying: "Oh, God, why, God? Get me on with life and to Kenya." All I wanted was an email from our agency that said: "Report to Nairobi next week." In my dreams I did cartwheels upon hearing these words. However, in real life, no email came. As a pastor for years, I'd counseled parishioners in hard spots such as this to believe "something good was coming," but, in the early months of 2013, I could not name anything good about my life other than Kevin and the few friends from far away that kept in touch.

On my saddest days of missing my friends and my church role back East, Kevin reminded me of our joint calling to Feed the Children. He'd pull out the rock and tell me the story again. "Don't you'd remember why we came here, Elizabeth?" For it was true, we both believed that God had led us as a family to pour our hearts into Feed the Children. We'd now seen firsthand what hungry kids looked like, and we wanted to be strong advocates for those we'd met and millions more like them. We knew Kevin's efforts to love the staff, tell the story of the good work, and raise money were making a difference. We knew the adoption would happen. Did we just need to learn patience?

Gloomy days or not, I kept going. It was now Lent, after all, the season of discipline. So, I pursued action. Any action. I started reading a chapter a night from the book of John, hoping to get a glimpse as to why following Jesus felt so hard. I forced myself to take afternoon walks around our neighborhood, listening to songs in my earbuds that Jean told me were among her favorites. I shopped at a local market almost daily for fresh meat and veggies for dinner. I took meetings with anyone in the city who might connect me to a ministry opportunity through which I could be useful. I volunteered more at Feed the Children, accompanying Kevin on international trips to the Philippines, Guatemala, and Nicaragua. In these places, I hugged babies. (*Thank you, Shiphrah, for making those moments possible.*) For weeks at a time, I handed out plates of tortillas, rice, and beans, and received homemade gifts of all kinds from kids so thankful that Feed the Children loved them. Without asking for it, my sabbatical gave me an advanced course in international development work and story writing. Soon I became "volunteer-in-chief" within Feed the Children's Public Relations and Communications department. I felt happiest on the road, doing something!

Still, any good I brought to the world by writing stories, loving kids and staff, and supporting Kevin's hectic pace at work still felt like a placeholder to me. It was a placeholder until motherhood—a placeholder until I could finally hold that Kenyan dear one in my arms and say, "I love you and will never let you go," just as Meredith had once done to me. I couldn't wait to settle down in our Northern Virginia home and have play dates with friends now birthing their second children. And, life felt like a placeholder till I could be a pastor again in a town that would accept me. Maybe I would only be able to work part-time, but Pastor Elizabeth and President Kevin with a Kenyan child felt like utopia—all I'd ever wanted, and more! Sure, a baby miraculously coming from my belly or with the support of Marie's eggs would be nice one day too. But, one thing at a time…Kenyan child first!

By July 2013, there was still no call from Kenya. Jean invited me to come and help her lead a week of summer camp in Tennessee. I needed to be close to anyone who loved me, and I think she understood that. When she told me I was in charge of nightly devotions for the adult counselors, I looked at her like she was crazy. *Me* speak? No one asked me to do that anymore. I didn't know whether it was still possible for me to put together a basic Bible study. Jean laughed at me, with a dumbfounded look on her face. However, in *my* mind, I thought that maybe my pastoral career had ended with our one big move across the country. The uncertainty bubble around our home made me question everything.

Back at home, I often cried "Why me, God?" tears and rolled around in piles of self-pity while watching pointless reality TV in bed. I wanted to be useful. I wanted to be a mother. And, in our minds, the August calendar page existed as an unofficial deadline of giving up hope. If nothing changed with our adoption process by that time, Kevin and I said we'd seriously consider doing something else. We had embryos waiting. I wanted to move home. We could not keep living in all-consuming limbo like this. Hadn't we suffered enough? Hadn't we been faithful enough? What was the hold-up? I didn't think life could feel any worse. But, of *course* it could! (*What was I thinking?*)

The second week of August, Kevin found me in our apartment unable to get out of bed, not from emotional pain, but the physical kind. The doc-in-a-box I'd visited the week before with some lower back issues informed me I had a kidney infection. I'd never had a kidney infection before, so I chalked up my discomfort to the normal part of the recovery process. However, one round of antibiotics later, the pain felt like sharp daggers slowly destroying my abdomen. Lying down, standing up, rolling over: any physical movement was out of the question. But, I'd experienced so much physical pain throughout the IVF process, I'd programmed myself not to complain. I told Kevin not to worry. This pain had to be normal.

But, by the second week, I was throwing up, not eating, and registering a high temperature. Kevin found my shoes and said, "We're going to the emergency room right now."

Within hours, an ultrasound revealed a different diagnosis from what we'd feared. We'd guessed I had either kidney stones or a ruptured appendix. Instead, the doctor said my right ovary contained a tumor. A very large tumor. *Seriously, of all the body parts that could be sick, it had to be this one?* Immediately, our minds wanted to connect the dots to our fertility treatments. Had all our years on hormones causes this? The doctor said no.

"Sometimes these things just happen. I hope it's not cancer, though."

Oh, dear God.

Kevin hardly had time to Google the doctor who took my case. Because the tumor measured the size of a small baby's head (*yes, really*), the nurses wheeled me into emergency surgery that night. I signed release forms in case the doctor needed to take my gall bladder, uterus, or more. Who knew how infected I was in there? I'd done the surgery thing so many times with all those egg removals, but this was obviously something different. No time to swap stories with others on Facebook who'd undergone similar procedures. *Thank God I was on morphine.* If what was really going on with me had registered with me, they might have needed to send me to the psych ward.

Without a church or anyone we knew in town other than people who worked for Kevin, my husband sat alone in the waiting room during the several-hour procedure. Eventually, his dear assistant, Patti, came to bring him something to eat and a change of clothes. She brought me a beautiful yellow blanket for when I woke up. When the surgery was over, with me hooked up to all kinds of tubes and wires, nurses monitored me in ICU for a while. The doctor—the one we'd just met—told Kevin I might not leave the hospital for days.

Night of terror, I tell you.

We'd have to wait days until the biopsy report could rule cancer out.

In the meantime, I feasted on Jello and pain medication while Kevin never left my side. I rocked the hospital booties. My room smelled amazing from the flowers our friends sent. When the biopsy came back on day three after surgery, I raised the arm without the IV in it, elated that I didn't have cancer. Finally, some good news, and we got to leave the hospital sooner than expected.

On the downside, I would face a two-month-plus recovery, unable to travel or take care of myself for a while. But, on a positive note: I retained an ovary and my uterus, the two parts

I needed both to be able to carry a baby and not to go into immediate menopause. The doctor tasked with my surgery told me pregnancy was still an option.

However, the surgery became the wretched gift that kept on giving. The hospital gave me a horrible stomach virus that turned into a major colon problem. Being able to eat again was something that only came slowly. The biggest accomplishment of my days became taking a shower and/or remembering to hug a pillow while coughing. But, on the upside, I lost weight. All of my stress-eating from the infertility years fell off easily when food wouldn't stay in my system. My mom, a trained nurse, came to help me learn to eat solid food again and to walk from my bed to the bathroom.

Days passed before I felt like turning on my computer, but, when I did, an even bigger shock came from a Kenyan email address: "We regret to inform you that the adoption board has denied your application for adoption."

What? Really…what? You've got to be kidding me.

The explanation accompanying the email amounted to a bunch of bologna. We allegedly hadn't sent an original copy of "X." (*They hadn't asked for it.*) We didn't verify this fact. (*They hadn't asked for that fact, either.*) I didn't have a job. (*How could I have a job when I was "on call" to go live in Kenya for 6–9 months?*)

Our case outcome stunned both the U.S. and Kenyan adoption agencies handling our case. "We've never seen this happen before," they both said in emails. "You did everything right!" Stunned silence fell over our eight hundred square foot loft apartment.

Did God hate us?

In my pajamas, on the couch, I thought a lot about why we had gone to all of this trouble for a year—yes, a whole year. Why had we wasted so much time? Why had we so easily allowed ourselves to be sucked into an international adoption journey in a country that had now rejected us?

The day of the email, I remained silent all day. Immobilized on my spot on the couch, I stared out of our floor-to-ceiling windows at the Oklahoma City skyline. I stared at the collection of house plants that friends had sent to remind me of the land of the living. I stared at my own hands battered from all the IVs, wondering: *Why? Just, Why?* My hospital stay had put Kevin behind at work, so I had lots of time alone as he caught up on essential projects.

When I emerged from the fog, I decided that I would never call this adoption a waste of time. I knew that fighting for a child to have a home where he/she knew two loving parents was never a waste of time. And, there was still hope. Our adoption agency said we could appeal. To my biggest objection of life feeling so unfair, I told myself, "Be positive. Stick with the recovery program. It's all you can do for now." Then, I went back to my 11:00 a.m. date with *The Price Is Right* with a sippy cup of ginger ale in my hand.

The horror of the unwanted news needed to work its way through me in its own time. It could not be rushed, nor could my recovery.

By the end of the year, I emerged from this scary medical situation all the more grateful to be alive, married to such a dear soul who took such great care of me, and in a phase of life and work when I was able to rest. It was also a bonus that no church's prayer list had to include a line that read: "Pastor Elizabeth: Recovering from her ovary removal" (*sooo TMI*).

My body healed a little more every day. I even received an invitation to preach for a week at a school conference in Hawaii. If that wasn't a bone of goodness thrown my way, I didn't know what was! For once in my life, being in a bathing suit on the beach felt like nothing compared to the stress I'd been through!

Through it all, I vowed that my first stop, post-recovery, would be at the fertility clinic. It was time for the embryos to go in! Though this baby to be would not technically be mine (and I wouldn't care if the world knew it), I rejoiced at the possibilities of him or her coming to life. I was more than ready now. I kept saying thank you to God for giving me an amazing friend such as Marie, *and* the modern technology of frozen embryos. Maybe 2014 would finally be our year?

With thankfulness for the human body's ability to heal itself, and my fertility doctor's endorsement, I signed up to complete IVF #9 at the beginning of 2014. To make this happen, I reacquainted myself with the routine of shots and pills, morning blood tests, and internal ultrasounds—all with the goal of positioning my body to receive the pregnancy at precisely the right time. I hated the process because of all the emotional triggers from past failures, of course, but I eagerly longed for the goal! Even better, I spent a month back in D.C. so I could be near our fertility clinic. And, on my birthday, my thirty-fourth birthday, we implanted two embryos—two of the four frozen ones we'd made with Marie.

The sisterhood came out in full support on that thirty-fourth birthday occasion. It just so happened that Jean already planned a trip for the weekend of my birthday. No longer did I call her my "former teacher." I loved Jean as a beloved adult friend. So, what a welcome relief that she sat with me on the couch, made another one of her glorious breakfasts the next day, and prayed with me about our desires for IVF to finally work! Meredith also called regularly to see how I was feeling, and Lucy checked in by text too. And, when a trip to El Salvador and Nicaragua was scheduled for Kevin including the day I was to find out whether or not I was pregnant, Marie booked a plane ticket in my direction. "You will not be alone," she declared.

Marie arrived hours before the time I knew the doctor might call with the results. I took her out for grilled cheese and tomato soup. We talked about how I would feel either way. Marie kept tapping her fingernails on the lunch counter. I could hardly eat half of the sandwich. Every minute my eyes kept going to my cell phone. When it finally rang at 2:17 p.m., I forced Marie to play Kevin's role of answering the phone. As I looked in her eyes, I knew from the first second of the phone call that the answer was no.

The treatment had failed, AGAIN.

You've got to be kidding me. Really?!?

Early the next morning, Marie needed to get home to her two babies and Bob. Hearing the sound of her pumping breast milk from our guest room did me no good either. And, as Feed the Children Nicaragua was still hosting Kevin for a couple more days, I stared into space. I ate little. And I counted the hours till Kevin returned home.

Emotionally, all hope chips landed in the adoption bucket. We'd appealed months earlier. But, within weeks, we'd learned that the Kenyan government would not accept our appeal. Fighters at heart, we appealed again. While we waited for the outcome, six months passed. Shiphrah remained hopeful it would all work out. I believed her. We'd all felt so called to this. I wanted to believe her. I kept myself busy by volunteering as much as I could at Feed the Children and picking up more freelance writing projects all the time. I made new friends within the organization that lightened my emotional load. But, truth be told, it was harder than ever to get out of bed. I was ready to give up on the placeholder.

Six months later, the Kenyan government issued a statement saying that no more foreign adoptions would be allowed. *Yes, really.* They were shutting down the entire international program. *Yes, really.* More months passed. We hung on to hope till the end, believing a case like ours "in process" might be still be processed. But, in the end, no. *Yes, really.*

The adoption would not happen. I repeat: the adoption would not happen.

But, I needed to find a way to keep living.

I faced the hard, cold truth that I had a life I did not want. I lived in a city and within an organizational system that still wasn't sure it liked me. I couldn't have or adopt children. In addition, people referred to me more days than not as "Kevin's wife." And there was nothing I could do about it, no matter how hard I tried. It was a pain from which I could not part, no matter what. Still, I continued to believe with every cell in my body I was meant to be a mother. I knew I would be a good mother. Holding all of those babies around the world did not take the desire from me. If anything, it made it stronger! The words of Psalm 37:4—a Bible verse I'd memorized as a child—stayed close in thought: "Take delight in the LORD, and God will give you the desires of your heart." Did God care at all about my desires? Or was it all a lie? I knew I faced two paths: hanging my head indefinitely as a "woe is me, life really crapped on me" person, or even now trusting in the resurrection promise I'd preached at countless funerals: "See, I am making all things new" (Rev. 21:5).

Which path would I choose? Hope, or bitterness?

For a long time, even those closest to me didn't know. The anger bubble in me wanted to explode. I kept it in check, mostly—though some days I didn't (sorry, Lucy!). Many months passed. No amount of books on grief (and boy, I read them all) or conversations with my counselor gave me the magic solution.

So, waiting on peace, I cried lots more tears. I sat up thinking in the middle of the night. I continued to throw baby announcements in the trash as soon as I recognized from the envelope that somebody else had sent me one. I wrote as little as I could. I went back on depression meds and sat in the realities of this dark, dark cloud of nine fertility fails and two failed adoptions. And, like anyone who's walked through a season of grief, small miracles happened every morning when I put one foot in front of the other in the direction of work, play, and friendship. I knew I topped the prayer lists of many who saw me move so slowly through daily tasks. When I hovered in bed extra long on weekday mornings, I thought a lot about how no one would miss me if I died. What did I have to offer the world anymore?

Shiphrah, way over in Kenya, became one of the weekly lifelines who kept me from falling deeper into a pit of despair. She kept reminding me to keep my chin up. She did not give up hope for brighter days for our household. "I know you will rise from this, Elizabeth," she said, over and over. Her optimism floored me. Mostly, I felt as if God really hated me—or, at least, that the Kenyan government did. I had letters of rejection to prove it!

Yet Shiphrah spoke often of God's mercies being new every morning. And she kept saying it to me over and over again. When I asked to her to explain further, she said one day over Skype, "God is a mystery beyond all comprehension. As much as we think we know God, we don't. Our lives truly begin the day we surrender all things back to our Creator." She gave me a book called *He Leadeth Me,* by Walter Ciszek, a memoir telling the story of a Jesuit priest sent to a Siberian work camp in Russia during World War II. Somehow my troubles seemed so much less dramatic when compared to Father Ciszek's time in prison and eleven years of hard labor. The book proved a spring board into deeper conversations about surrender.

One day I asked her, "Do you think God wants us to offer up what we want more than anything?" I asked.

"My dear, *yes*! Look at Jesus."

Oh, yes, Jesus, the one who gave his very life! Oh, Jesus who said, "No one has greater love than this, to lay down one's life for one's friends" (Jn. 15:13). I claimed to follow this man. But did I *really?* Now, it felt so much more serious.

She went on, "And why do you make this suffering so personal? Why do you say God did this to you? Why do you say the Kenyan government hates you?"

"Because it does!" I protested.

"No, it doesn't. And God loves you more than you'll ever know, my dear. Nothing about that has ever changed, though your circumstances might feel that way now."

I sighed.

"And Kenya. Don't say that Kenya hates you. Kenya is a beautiful country, God's country. Don't you love it here?"

"I do. That is why I wanted to have a Kenyan child so much!"

She went on, "Evil wins, my dear, when we make suffering so personal. Open your eyes and see the world as God sees it. Sure, this situation has not turned out as we'd hoped, but it doesn't mean the story is over. It's okay if we don't understand."

It took time to accept what Shiphrah offered. Weeks turned into months. But, slowly, I began to trust the deep font of wisdom she carried. It came from a woman who loved me like I was one of her own.

So, maybe I would not have a family in the way I had always planned. However, because I was still breathing, wasn't there still hope?

Shiphrah, whose name means "beauty" in Hebrew, continued to teach me perspective. One day she asked me on the phone: "Why do you say 'I *must* have a child'?"

"Because this is my deep desire and no matter how I try to make it go away, it doesn't."

She offered: "Maybe one day you will, Elizabeth. God is full of amazing surprises. Don't you see? All of life is a gift. There's nothing about life that you or I deserve. Nothing."

My stomach churned. I was really listening. I hated it, but I knew she was right. All of life is a gift. Who was I to say I deserved anything? Not in a self-demeaning sort of way, but from remembering the character of God. God's mercies *are* new every morning (Lam. 3:22–23). And, *this* is where I needed to ground myself before anything could come next.

Maybe, one day, we'd enter another adoption process? Maybe. Maybe, one day, we'd try IVF again with those other two frozen embryos? Maybe. Or, maybe not. Hadn't the fertile community around my life taught me anything? God knew me. God knew what I needed. God would not forget my desires! Yet, surrender was the only way forward. And, if I didn't want bitterness to lodge in my soul, I needed to say yes again to God even while everything in my life felt in shambles.

And, if I still wanted to be on the journey to birth myself and live into the wisdom that my spiritual guides offered, then I needed to let go of my timetable and the particularities of my dreams of motherhood. I needed to ask God to give me strength to dream in the present tense. And, it was okay if I didn't have a clue as to what these dreams would be, or who would show up (or not) as companions. My soul still resided in the delivery room, waiting and anticipating. The exact place it belonged.

If you are throwing the book across the room right now, I totally understand. This story (and my life) is not ending up how I ever thought it would be.

But, I'm still around to write it (a miracle). I still believe in the goodness of God (another miracle). And, I'm telling my new congregation that loves me in Oklahoma that God's mercies are new every morning (a double miracle). A divine pastor-congregation match surprised me in August 2014. The loveliest church on the western plains called me their pastor and said, "Welcome home!"

Several months later on Easter Sunday, I gave testimony to the day years before when I told God, "I'm not sure I believe in you," after a series of our devastating losses. I shared with them that within seconds of those words leaving my lips, the Spirit touched me as it did with Mary at the tomb, saying: "I don't appreciate your non-acknowledgment of me. You can say and do a lot of things, but you can't forget I'm here and always will be." I preached that resurrection always comes in the unique parts of their stories, as it did in mine. The glory of God is that we are people of the resurrection! New life is always possible. Always.

Many parishioners told me later it was one of the best Easter sermons they'd ever heard. Every bit of it came from the contours, rubs, and grooves of my own tear-stained journey. And I couldn't have been prouder to offer it to *them*. I believed every word.

My birth story has only just begun.

Afterword

Without realizing it, one day I crossed into new territory: my life was no longer focused on having a baby. It wasn't because my desire to mother went away. It wasn't because I'd made peace with my childless status *as some encouraged me to do all along.* And it wasn't because a fertility treatment or adoption proceeding actually found its way into the success check box. Kevin and I were parents. We just were. I had more children in my life than I ever could have imagined when the journey began. And these children had nothing to do with Kevin's employment status or the number of people living in our home. Or even the beloved nephews that filled some of our free time with such joy. But, how?

Kevin's contract with Feed the Children concluded in May of 2015 meaning our official relationship with this organization that we loved (and me, my new beloved church in Oklahoma) ended. But, we quickly learned that work of parenting kids all over the world would continue. We just couldn't spend Christmas and Thanksgivings and celebrate birthdays with children in orphanages and walk away. Bonds like these are for life.

But I most want to tell you about this: in August 2015, a heart-to-heart conversation with a dear friend opened my eyes to the importance of solidifying all of this kind of mothering in a particular direction.

"When are you going to start something, Elizabeth?" she said, "There's no question in my mind that you need to, the way you talk about your kids. And my husband and I are ready to support you when you do." The light shone brightly in that moment. I heard. There was no way not to do something after that. And this something came in the form of a foundation. I would start a foundation.

In the birthing process of this non-profit I thought a lot about the hopes of children like Martha, Godfrey and Juan that I loved. I wondered how I could come alongside them and support their dreams? How could our friends do the same, and churches too? I really wanted to put my love toward action. I wanted be a good steward of all the non-profit wisdom around us to be able to encourage children's homes. And this was what the birthing process came down to: the start of Our Courageous Kids. Our Courageous Kids would provide grants for education and life enrichment activities for kids living in centers like those we'd encountered through our Feed the Children years. For this reality hovered closely to me: children like Faith, Sarah and Julis belong to us all (and by all I mean you reading this book right now). If we don't champion them who will? Children deserve more than what even the best centers provide—they deserve the same opportunities for secondary education and college readily available to the kids living down the street from me in the US.

So, with all of the necessary 501(c) 3 paperwork now completed, I look forward to awarding some of my first grants by the end of 2016 to assist several high school girls with school and counseling fees and possibly another boy to go to college. I want to be a resource to orphanages when the needs for their older kids overwhelm them. And I can't wait to get to know so many more beloved brave ones as this new work unfolds. I don't just want to encourage donors to write checks, but rather to join me in the experience of knowing kids all over the world. The family of God is bigger than we really know. To learn more, visit www.ourcourageouskids.org

And so are the surprises in life especially as this book went to print. My kitchen counter is now covered in pacifiers and formula. An infant carrier is now strapped into the backseat of my car. And like years ago, in our bedroom there is a steady stream of crying in the middle of the night, but this time it's easily soothed by a bottle or a diaper change. My arms are full and my soul, though tired, is flooded with joy. My global family bursting with children is more than enough.

Acknowledgments

To all our friends and family—both far and near—who have loved us, prayed for us, and sat with us through these darkest nights: "Thank you" hardly seems to be enough. You saw beyond our pain and dreamed when we could not. You raised up both me and this book!

To our church family during most of the events unfolding in this story, Washington Plaza Baptist Church in Reston, Virginia: Though you may not have known what was brewing below the surface of your pastor's heart, you loved me, wet hair and all. Jane Tatum, Ernie Brunson, Mary and Craig Mass, Ken Williamson and Barbara Schipper: You got me through some of my toughest days in life and ministry, whether you knew it or not.

To the members of the Federated Church in Weatherford, Oklahoma, for pulling me back into the pulpit where I belong so I could live out resurrection with you, and to Edith Guffey for making this life-changing match happen. Weatherford, I will always love you.

To the Writing Revs who first invited me to join them in 2010: Ruth Everhart, Leslie Klingensmith, MaryAnn McKibben Dana, Carol Howard Merritt, Susan Graceson, and then Martha Spong and Barbara Meloch, who came to our group later: You gave me courage to dream of this day. And, with every draft you read, you gave me bravery to say (and really mean it): "I'm a writer," so I could finish the last chapters of the book!

To the Collegeville Institute for giving me valuable space to think and reflect during a writing workshop in Minnesota in 2010, and for the loveliest of colleagues who offered such valuable feedback.

To the Louisville Institute for offering me the Pastoral Study Grant project award in 2011. Your generous support of this idea gave me both the financial resources I needed to wri a concentrated amount of time and to be filled up with cou to bare my soul.

To all of those who graciously received emails from me w instructions "to read a chapter (or more) and tell me what yc think" and then provided great insight and grammar lesson along the way: Gail Kearney, Amy Butler, Beth Dotson, Abby Thornton Hailey, Ellis Duncan, Kristina Everingham, Lawren Bercaw, Britta Eastburg, J. Dana Trent, Joy Bennett, Susan Smartt Cook, Charlotte Rogers, Terry Magill, Alice Stanton, and Tamara Perry-Lunardo.

To the team at Chalice Press: What a delight you are! You saw the potential in this project and welcomed me so warmly. I'm one of your biggest fans!

And, most of all, to the man who fought for me, fought for our marriage, and embodies a deep belief that the best is yet to come. It takes a real man to allow such a personal story of ours to belong to the world, when at heart you're much more private. But here we are together taking this leap. I love you, Kevin Hagan, with all my heart. And, friends of this book, you should too!

...ted Resources

...irs

...n's *Triumph over Despair and Statistics* by Julia ...rk: Broadway Books, 2001.

...*rning Hopeful Dreams into New Beginnings* by Sheridan ...lle: Thomas Nelson, 2013.

...*ile and Addicted to Hope* by Tertia Loebenberg Albetyn. ...rg: Porcupine Press, 2009.

on Child Loss

...*ther: Journeys through Perinatal Bereavement*, ed. Joy M. Freedman Tabatha D. Johnson. Valley Forge, Pennsylvania.: Judson Press, ...16.

...*ugh the Darkness Gather Round: Devotions about Infertility, Miscarriage, and Child Loss*, ed. Mary Elizabeth Hill Hatchey and Erin K. McClain. Macon, Georgia: Smyth and Helwys, 2015.

What Was Lost: A Christian Journey through Miscarriage by Elise Erikson Barrett. Louisville: Westminster John Knox, 2011.

Blogs within the Infertility Community

Amateur Nester: Inspiration and Encouragement During Infertility. www.amateurnester.com

Ever Upward. www.everupward.org

Resolve: The National Infertility Association. www.resolve.org

Embracing Darkness and Grief

Lament for a Son by Nicholas Wolterstorff. Grand Rapids: Wm. B. Eerdmans, 1987.

Learning to Walk in the Dark by Barbara Brown Taylor. New York: Harper Collins, 2014.

Stations of the Heart: A Parting of a Son by Richard Lischer. New York: Vintage, 2013.

Stitches: A Handbook of Meaning, Hope and Repair by Anne Lamott. New York: Riverhead Books, 2013.

Surrendering Your Life to the Unknown

He Leadeth Me by Walter Ciszek, S.J., with Daniel Flaherty. New York: Random House, 2012 (originally published in 1973).

Poustinia: Encountering God in Silence, Solitude and Prayer by Catherine de Hueck Doherty. Combermere, Ontario: Madonna House, 3d ed., 2014.

Ruthless Trust: The Ragamuffin's Path to God by Brennan Manning. New York: Harper Collins, 2009.